TO JACK & BARBARA –
THIS IS A STORY ABOUT A CRAZY GERMAN GUY WHO MET A BRAZILIAN BEAUTY AND STARTED TELEVISION ON THE WEST COAST. ENJOY!

LINE of SIGHT

Klaus Landsberg -- His Life and Vision

Evelyn De Wolfe &

George Lewis

LINE of SIGHT

Klaus Landsberg -- His Life and Vision

By Evelyn De Wolfe & George Lewis

ISBN 978-1530946953
ISBN -1530946859
LCCN 2016905815

The Ashlin Press

Hollywood, California, USA

CreateSpace Independent Publishing Platform
North Charleston, South Carolina

Copies available at
Amazon.com, Amazon Europe, CreateSpace and
www.readevelyn.com

The Authors invite any copyright holders they have not been able to reach, to contact them so that full acknowledgment may be given in subsequent editions.

Klaus Landsberg

FOREWORD

The first regularly scheduled television service in America began on April 30, 1939, when NBC and its parent RCA showed President Franklin Roosevelt opening the World's Fair from Flushing Meadows, New York.

One of the pioneers who realized TV's possibilities was twenty-three-year-old Klaus Landsberg, who was toiling with NBC at the time. By 1941 he was in Los Angeles working for Paramount Pictures, tasked with creating a television operation from scratch. That station eventually became KTLA channel 5, the first commercial TV station west of the Mississippi.

Klaus believed in taking his cameras everywhere, bringing into viewers' homes live pictures of news, sports and entertainment of all kinds, wherever they were happening.

The motto of the station was "See It Best, See It Live on KTLA Channel Five!" The letters K-T-L-A stood for Kilocycles Television Los Angeles, but closer to the truth would have been Klaus Television Landsberg Associates.

This is the never before told story of one of the dreamers who defined Television.

Joel Tator*

**Joel Tator produced and directed more than 8,500 broadcasts and collected 25 Emmy awards along the way.*

CONTENTS

Foreword ... vii
Contents ... ix
Acknowledgements ... xi
Preface ... xiii

Chapter 1 – Mile-High Proposal ... 1
Chapter 2 – Let the Games Begin ... 13
Chapter 3 – Passport to Freedom ... 29
Chapter 4 – Go West Young Man ... 39
Chapter 5 – Performing Without a Net ... 49
Chapter 6 – Tying the Knot ... 61
Chapter 7 – Opening Night ... 73
Chapter 8 – Deadly Brew ... 83
Chapter 9 – Who's on First ... 89
Chapter 10 –Everyone's Child ... 99
Chapter 11 –The Dream Team ... 111
Chapter 12 –The Breakup ... 121
Chapter 13 –They Said It Couldn't Be Done ... 135
Chapter 14 –When the Earth Shook ... 151
Chapter 15 –Bittersweet Sunday ... 161
Chapter 16 –The Legacy ... 167

Source Notes ... 177
About Evelyn De Wolfe ... 185
About George Lewis ... 187

ACKNOWLEDGMENTS

As coauthors of *Line of Sight: Klaus Landsberg—His Life and Vision*, George Lewis and I wish to thank those who so generously contributed inspiration and knowledge in creating this book.

To my son Cleve Landsberg, for urging me to share my memories of his father and enriching our research, and to my able partner George Lewis for joining me on this project.

To my parents for preserving letters, I sent them after leaving my native Brazil and during my marriage to Klaus. They enabled me to relive, with freshness and clarity, the formative years of West Coast television that were so much a part of my young adult life.

To Klaus's parents and his brother Peter Landsberg for sharing family history, and Klaus's early progress as a promising engineer and inventor.

George's special thanks go to the love of his life and chief muse, Cecilia Alvear, a former NBC News producer, whose suggestions about the copy and whose company on research trips were invaluable.

We are grateful for the oral histories obtained from Klaus's co-workers—John Polich, Roy White, John Silva, Robin Clark, Stan Chambers, Bob Reagan, Dick Lane, Eddie Resnick, Sherman

Loudermilk and countless others who shared their personal reminiscences in separate interviews.

To Joel Tator, a heartfelt thank you for his zeal in documenting KTLA's history and for inviting me to participate in its anniversary specials. To the late Bruce Cohn for initially brainstorming various aspects of this book, and to the late Syd Cassyd, founder of the Academy of Television Arts and Sciences, for sharing his early recollections. To Jackie McDonnell Smith for photos and Chris Northrup for valuable contacts. Further thanks to Nora Bates of the Television Academy Foundation.

Most especially, we are indebted to Jay Christopher Horak, Patt Morrison, Joe Saltzman and Morrie Gelman, for taking the time to read our work, and allowing us to place excerpts of their comments on the back cover.

Last but not least, to the man himself, Klaus, whose uniqueness most inspired this book.

***

PREFACE

Shortly after arriving in the United States in 1943, wide-eyed and twenty-one, I met a young Berliner who had escaped from Nazi Germany five years before with an invention that would open doors for him in America.

The world was at war. America was bonded to its Allies, willing to fight on foreign soil and endure whatever sacrifices would help strike down Fascism. Such songs as "Pistol Packin' Mama", "Paper Doll," "White Christmas" were born in that time, and two classic films, *Casablanca* and *For Whom the Bell Tolls* were nominated for the Academy of Motion Picture Arts and Sciences Oscar Award.

These were oppressive but impelling days when patriotism was at an all-time high in America. The Stars and Stripes flew proudly, and the words of Gen. Dwight D. Eisenhower, "Beware the fury of an aroused democracy,"stirred this nation.

Klaus Landsberg was busy helping to usher in the new era of television, regarded by the US government as a potentially important technology in its defense arsenal – a new industry destined to change popular culture forever.

In its infancy in the 1930's and 40s, television was an eager performer waiting impatiently in the wings to take center stage. World

War II got in the way, halted the production of receiving sets, and delayed the introduction of commercial telecasting. But thanks to the grit and ingenuity of relentless young pioneers like Landsberg, the new medium was fully ready to blossom on both coasts in the booming postwar years.

Klaus's passion for his work, his brilliance, and his dedication mesmerized me. When he asked me to marry him, I didn't hesitate, never suspecting that television would become a demanding mistress, monopolize every aspect of his life, and eventually break up our marriage.

Most histories of American television have centered on what the big networks in New York were doing in those early years. Moreover, the chroniclers, for the most part, were oblivious to what was happening west of the Mississippi. A lot *was* happening.

To date, no real portrait exists of this immigrant trailblazer who accomplished so much in so short a lifespan. He died of cancer at the age of forty. Little is known of his early struggles, his dramatic escape from Nazi Germany, his love affair with Lady Liberty, his fascination with free enterprise, and his belief that television could become the greatest tool for learning.

Often described as part Edison, part P.T. Barnum, Klaus was both scientist and showman -- a driven man equally adept at solving complex engineering problems as he was discovering new talent and creating innovative program concepts. With his handpicked *dream team,* he provided ringside seats for his loyal viewers at sports arenas, political clambakes, and big-band ballrooms. And he demonstrated, as never before, with live coverage of noteworthy events, how compelling television was in transporting its viewers to the scene and the moment of a breaking news story.

As KTLA's founder, its general manager, and Paramount Television's vice-president, Klaus produced and personally directed more than 3,500 TV shows. In the industry, he was both lionized and disliked, yet even his sharpest critics showed unusual allegiance and respect for this multi-talented man who never asked more of anyone than of himself. He accomplished challenging "firsts" that others said couldn't be done. In his time he was described as the "*wunderkind*", "the golden boy of television." and "one of the single most important factors in the making of television history in the West". As his first wife, I had a backstage pass to that amazing world of Klaus Landsberg.

In a fortunate collaboration with fellow journalist George Lewis, a highly-honored former NBC news correspondent and technology buff, we hope this joint effort contributes not only an eyewitness's perspective of the formative years of West Coast television but also reveals some of the silliness, pathos, joys, conflicts, humor and vulnerability that belong in an honest portrayal of an individual worth knowing.

For Klaus, "Line of Sight" was more than just a TV technical term. It was his path of unobstructed vision about what could be, and what should be that still resonates for us today.

Evelyn De Wolfe

The two of us on Mt. Wilson

CHAPTER 1

A Mile-High Proposal

Some men express their love in unique ways, as I was about to find out when Klaus Landsberg drove me to the top of Mount Wilson in the fall of 1944.

Original W6XYZ transmitter site on Mt. Wilson

Standing 5,710 feet above the Los Angeles basin, the mountaintop is a serene spot with a commanding view of most of Southern California. On a clear day, you can see from Santa Barbara almost to the Mexican border. It's the place where, in the early part of the 20th century, eminent astronomers like Edwin Hubble gazed at the stars through the telescopes of the Mount Wilson Observatory. It's also the place Klaus picked to locate the transmitter for the experimental television station W6XYZ, owned by Paramount Pictures, a choice that seemed rather fitting for a movie studio that uses a mountain as its logo.

As we reached the summit, all I could see was a solitary antenna tower and the two-story building that housed the station's transmitter and living quarters. In the wintertime, this could be a very isolated spot with heavy snowfalls blocking the roads and eighty-five-mile-an hour gusts of wind blasting the top of the mountain. Klaus had been tinkering with that antenna, updating and strengthening it to survive the elements.

It was so exciting to share all this with the man I loved, most of all feeling his passion for technology and what he hoped to do with it. He was anxious to see how construction was progressing on the new tower and wanted me to meet Ray "Pappy" Moore, his good friend and chief engineer, charged with the care and maintenance of the transmitter.

Ray was a cheerful Irishman, who took everything in stride though his job required him to lead a monastic life on top of the mountain for a week at a stretch, separated from his family. I would later meet Ray's wife Barbara, his two young sons and his mother Catherine, and a close relationship between our families would evolve.

With a broad smile, Klaus suggested that if we went to the very top of the tower, I would see what he meant by television's primary need for a good "line of sight." He persuaded me to climb into a bucket-like contraption suspended from a cable with pulleys and counterweights. At the opposite end, there was a hand-cranked winch and, with great gusto, Ray began turning a wheel on it and hoisting us to the top of the tower.

They say that love conquers all, so I guess it was love that enabled me to overcome my fear of heights as I stood in that swaying bucket, clinging to Klaus for dear life. Meanwhile, Ray kept cranking us farther up that tower, inch by inch.

Klaus was in heaven, filling his lungs with the fresh mountain air, pointing enthusiastically in different directions to show me why he had chosen this particular peak for his transmitting antenna. His eyes sparkled.

"From this height we have the farthest line of sight," he said, "farther than any competing station, anywhere. Wait and see; someday they'll all want to be on this mountain."

Klaus was right. Today, high above the Douglas firs and the Coulter pines of the Angeles National Forest stands another forest—one made up of steel spires. More than two dozen antenna towers that transmit the signals for most of the television and FM radio stations in Los Angeles are now there. They remind me of a famous LA landmark – Simon Rodia's Watts Towers—although the Mount Wilson version is like Rodia's creation, only replicated and magnified over and over.

In his precise way, Klaus explained to me that over-the-air television signals behave much like light waves. "Unlike radio waves, they travel in a straight path from the transmitter to the receiver. They can't bend around the curvature of the Earth, so transmissions are limited to the visible horizon—the line of sight."

Before Hollywood came calling, Klaus had worked in New York where the first TV broadcasters were busy placing their antennas on top of the Empire State Building. He knew that here, from this mountaintop, he could beam his signal almost 100 miles in every direction, compared to the forty- to fifty-mile range of the New York stations.

Reaching as far as we could go up that tower, feeling safe in his protective embrace, I soon discovered Klaus had an ulterior motive for bringing me up there. More about that later.

A Twist of Fate

So how was it that a young man from Germany and a young woman from Brazil were brought together for this romantic "summit meeting" in Southern California? The answer is partly a consequence of World War II and partly because of my curiosity about Hollywood.

In my hometown of Rio de Janeiro, I was working as a translator for the Coordinator of Inter-American Affairs and the US Office of Strategic Services photo unit. It was exciting working alongside director John Ford and cinematographer Gregg Toland and being an interpreter for such visitors as Walter Winchell, Orson Welles, Bernard Baruch, at a time when the United States was courting Brazil as its wartime ally. American planes, ships, men, and materials were reaching North Africa from air bases built on Brazil's northeastern land – a location that became known as the "Springboard for Victory."

I came to the United States in December of 1943 on a student/teacher fellowship to the University of Washington, as one of 416 foreign visitors studying at American universities under the auspices of the Institute of International Education. My itinerary had me traveling from Florida to Washington State with a two-week stopover in Los Angeles, where I expressed a desire to see how they made Hollywood movies. My host, Brazilian Consul Raul Bopp, arranged for a tour of Paramount Studios.

It was there that I noticed a door with a sign: "Experimental Television Station W6XYZ." The word "experimental" always intrigued me, conjuring up images of scientists in lab coats, bent over emerging discoveries.

"What is television?" I asked the young man guiding us around the lot. He chuckled and said, "To tell you the truth, I haven't the faintest idea. Only one person knows for sure – that's the man behind that door."

The man's name, he said, was Klaus Landsberg, a German genius who was developing some technical system for Paramount. "They say it lets people see what's happening somewhere else, without being there. Something crazy like that. Would you like to meet him?"

"I'd love to," I said.

We knocked. A slender young man, of medium height, brown eyes and light brown hair—certainly not the bearded, bespectacled scientist I had expected—opened the door. Our guide explained I was visiting from Brazil and was curious to know about television.

Klaus seemed delighted by our interest and invited us into his small domain. I was immediately struck by his radiant smile more than by his Spartan surroundings.

"This is the least glamorous part of Paramount Studios," he apologized, "but some very exciting things are happening here. I'm so glad when people show an interest in what we are doing. It'll be huge in the future," he added, in what would turn out to be a monumental understatement.

Longtime TV critic Cecil Smith of the *Los Angeles Times* later wrote of Klaus: "He believed television was a God-given instrument on which one could watch the world happen. It was his mission in life to make it work."

The tiny space assigned to Paramount's experimental TV station occupied part of an old still-photo set. It was divided into two areas—the "stage," a gray cloth backdrop that concealed an assortment of props, equipment, and charts, and the "control booth" next to a few rows of chairs. Newlyweds Lucille Ball and Desi Arnaz occasionally occupied those seats, and I later wondered if they may have drawn some inspiration for their *I Love Lucy* show from watching W6XYZ's weekly sitcom *Embarrassing Situations*, featuring a married couple.

Klaus led us up narrow wooden steps to his loft office and introduced us to his assistant, Claudia. "This is Evelyn Ashlin from Rio de Janeiro and Mr. Bopp, the Brazilian consul. Evelyn is interested in our work, and I'd like her to have one of our new program schedules." Claudia handed me a small blue and gray mailer with the words "NEWS FROM W6XYZ."

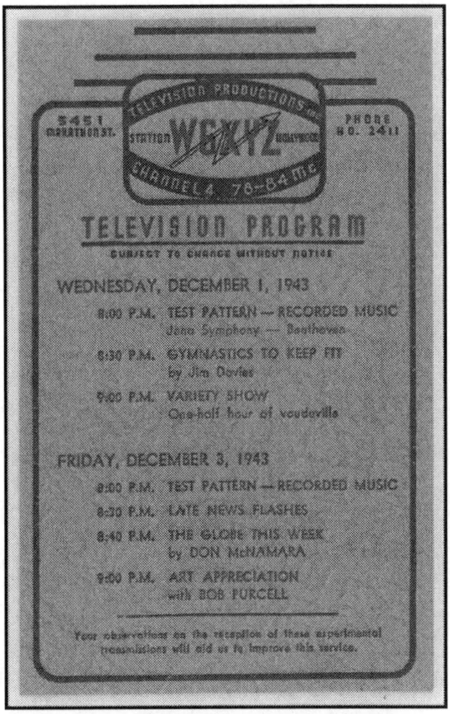

1943 schedule for W6XYZ

"They're just off the presses," said Klaus proudly, "and you are the first to receive one. We'll be mailing them out regularly to L.A.'s three hundred TV-set owners. Our viewers are contributing to our experiment. They report to us on the clarity of our images, and it helps us improve our transmission.

"But now I'd like to know more about Brazil," he continued. "Could we talk over dinner tonight?"

"I don't think I can, tonight," I said, hoping Klaus would insist. In those days, a young lady was taught not to appear too eager to accept an invitation from a man she'd just met.

"So, how about tomorrow night?" he asked.

"Maybe," I replied coyly.

His eyes smiled. "I don't have time for maybes, but I do make time for things that are important to me."

We were flirting. "In that case, Mr. Landsberg, tomorrow night, if Mr. Bopp will agree to join us."

"With pleasure," said the consul. "I'll bring my fiancée."

The next night, Klaus took us to the old Lucey's restaurant close to Paramount Studios, not to be confused with Lucy's El Adobe down the street, a current hangout for actors.

At Lucey's, I spotted the lovely Lana Turner in her trademark tight-fitting sweater and at a nearby table two rising stars, Kirk Douglas, and Burt Lancaster. A stunning brunette stopped by our table, and Klaus introduced her. She was Yvonne de Carlo, a starlet he said he'd been dating, and whose film career would soon flourish.

Klaus suggested we order whatever we wished since we were VIPs from Brazil, and he could charge it to his expense account. His unassuming ways enchanted me. His voice was deep and sexy, with just a slight German accent, but what impressed me the most was what he had to say. He spoke of his work with such joy, sounding more like a little kid to whom television was a grand Tinkertoy with endless possibilities.

The dinner lasted three hours. And while our companions seemed quite involved in their romantic tête-à-tête, Klaus and I, both newcomers to this country, were discovering how much we had in common, in spite of our diverse backgrounds. The time spent over dinner was truly magical.

Two days later, I boarded the train for Seattle, to experience American college life some ten thousand miles away from my hometown of Rio de Janeiro. While I'd met Klaus only briefly, he and his work fascinated me, and I hoped we would meet again someday. Little did I suspect that our futures would soon be linked.

I wrote him from Seattle.

The best friendships in the world have risen from fleeting moments full of depth. I believe our conversations scratched the surface of deeper understanding, and I greet you, my friend.

I often think of that wonderful plan you had in mind to use television as a medium for educating illiterate masses. I believe this plan is of tremendous scope, and if carried out would bring great benefit to countries like my own. I haven't yet written about it to my country because I have insufficient information about your concept, and it has been so long since we talked about it.

There is a possibility I may be coming to Los Angeles when the second semester is over to work on a US government radio program to South America, involving NBC and Paramount. If I do go, I'd like to talk to you more about your ideas for television.

It's been interesting being a young faculty member at such a large University and giving many speeches on South America. Now and then, I have escaped to the snowy mountains, since it would be a pity if I did not try skiing at least once in my life. Had a grand time but almost broke my neck. Also tried bowling and badminton and cycled all the way to Canada.

Klaus replied.

I envy you greatly for having had a chance to go skiing. It is one of my favorite sports; the other is sailing. I was such a slave of my work this past winter that I couldn't manage to get away for even one weekend to go up into the mountains. But then again, as you know, I love my work. It is not work to me but stimulation and enjoyment.

Television to me is so much more than what Hollywood sees in it, and I'm so possessed of ideas and ideals about it that the phoniness that surrounds me bothers me little. How much more would I look forward to your spending some time down here, the only danger being that I might not want you to leave at all. I'm convinced we should be able to do better than scratch the surface of understanding.

A Paramount movie contract also lured me back to Hollywood, but the offer to work for Walt Disney on war-related film projects enticed me more. Walt Disney sent me to New Mexico as his representative to test two versions of a literacy program he designed to strengthen relations with Latin America. He also asked me to report on sanitation conditions in the state's rural communities. Both assignments were right up my alley since I was a bilingual teacher and had done volunteer work in health care in the "favelas" of Rio.

Meanwhile, my romance with Klaus was blossoming. While on my three-week assignment for Disney, I received letters from him each day—all exuberantly romantic and filled with admiration and devotion for me. I may not have lived up to his expectations, but it felt good being on a pedestal. He often seemed so like a child in need of understanding, reassurance, and praise.

Being a hopeless paper packrat, and having always held on to old letters, I'm fortunate to be able to retrieve much of the zest and freshness of bygone memories.

Klaus wrote:

Darling, if only it could be possible for us to work together. It is not only the constant stimulation I receive from you mentally as well as emotionally.

It is not only with such devotion I dedicate my work to you, but Baby I now demand much more from myself than before. Your thoughts and ideas combined with mine make our work what it is and will make us accomplish so much more than we could do alone!

Goethe says it so beautifully: "there is a great difference between sharing somebody's life and sharing his thoughts. You can live in some people though not with them. Only the purest love and friendship can do both!"

Klaus believed that doing research and inventing would never be enough.

We must see to it that what we develop is used for what we know it should be used. We must guide the application of the tools we produce and the two of us, together as one, can do it. We are not doing research for research's sake but because we want to find something we feel is needed. I could've kept on working in the laboratory all my life but had my good reasons for leaving it.

His letters always ended with the words, "I will always, in all ways, and with all my love be your Klaus."

So there we were, dangling in a bucket together at the top of that TV tower when Klaus finally revealed his romantic and somewhat nerdy intent for hoisting me up that steel contraption. With a broad grin on his face, he popped the question.

"Will you marry me?"

There was only one answer to such a lofty proposal.

"YES."

***

CHAPTER 2

Let the Games Begin

On August 1, 1936, Adolf Hitler stood in Berlin's *Olympiastadion* – the Olympic Stadium – before a throng of 100,000 spectators and 3,963 athletes representing 49 nations.

Adolf Hitler opens the 1936 Berlin Olympics

He opened the Games of the XI Olympiad with the Nazi salute, and thousands in the audience responded in kind. On that day, Hitler, with the help of his propaganda machine, tried to showcase Nazi Germany as a welcoming place.

His advisors persuaded him that with the whole world watching, it might be wise to ignore the anti-homosexual laws that were normally so vigorously enforced. It might also be wise to round up the gypsies who lived in Berlin streets and keep them out of sight.

In his classic book *The Rise and Fall of the Third Reich*, William L. Shirer wrote: "The signs '*Juden Unerwuenscht'* (Jews Not Welcome) were quietly hauled down from the shops, hotels, beer gardens and places of public entertainment. The persecution of the Jews and the two Christian churches temporarily halted, and the country put on its best behavior."

Hitler chose a state-of-the-art technology to help enhance his image–something called "*Fernsehen*" (television). It would be the first time in history that the Olympics would be broadcast on TV, and the Nazis bragged about their accomplishment with a propaganda booklet prepared for the occasion. In it, they trumpeted their advances in the field of television, calling the Third Reich's contributions "a cultural development that promises to be of unsuspected importance to mankind."

The Germans liked to think they had a major hand in inventing television. In 1884, a German scientist named Paul Nipkow demonstrated a mechanical scanning disk that would later pave the way for the first crude television transmissions. The British advanced the technology when John Logie Baird gave the world's first demonstration of true television in 1926 before fifty scientists in an attic room in central London. There were others. However, it was an American, Philo Farnsworth, and a Russian immigrant to the United States, Vladimir Zworykin, who developed the first all-electronic television systems that replaced mechanical scanning in the 1930's.

At the Olympics, the TV gear was so new and untested that it required a gaggle of wizards to keep it going. In their eagerness to experiment with this new medium, the Germans had cobbled together a collection of equipment that combined homegrown gadgets with devices imported from other countries. They used three different systems to cover the games, two of them employing American "live" camera technology developed by Zworykin at RCA and Farnsworth at his Philadelphia laboratory.

The third one, known as the *Zwischenfilm* system, was a marvel of Teutonic ingenuity, partly electronic, partly mechanical. The Germans used a thirty-five-millimeter motion picture camera mounted on a van to record the action with the film running through a light-tight tube to a developing machine inside the vehicle. The film would be processed in ninety seconds and then projected on a scanning device that turned the pictures into electronic signals. This provided another television first: re-runs. The film could be replayed repeatedly.

For the opening ceremony, the first big live broadcast, four trucks were set up outside the stadium to process the signal—one to receive the image, one to transmit audio, one to transmit video and one to control the quality of the image.

Inside those trucks, pioneering engineers were manipulating the picture as best they could. One of them was a twenty-year-old Jewish kid from Berlin named Klaus Landsberg, whose reputation in technology was such that his Nazi bosses may have deliberately ignored his heritage when they assigned him to the Olympics.

The Germans set up more than two dozen viewing rooms where the TV coverage could be watched on large screens in hotels and public halls. Some critics complained that the quality wasn't great, with screens that were small and pictures that were dim and fuzzy by today's standards. One New York journalist wrote, "Only the polo games show up fairly clearly when black or chestnut ponies are used."

Chancellor Hitler planned to use the games as a showcase for the superiority of the master race; the Pure Arians he was sure would win over any competitors. And his favorite filmmaker, Leni Riefenstahl, was on hand to record the anticipated victories for later showings in movie theaters.

However, Hitler's expectations for Olympic glory at the Berlin games fell short of his mark.

An American black man with spring-loaded legs—Jesse Owens—would beat his master race competitors in the 100- and 200-

meter sprints, the 4 x 100 relay, and the long jump winning four gold medals. The embarrassed Hitler did not want to shake this "inferior" man's hand, as was the custom for national leaders at the Olympic Games, and he avoided a public-relations disaster by not shaking the hands of any medal winners.

Jesse Owens goes for the gold

After the Olympic flame was extinguished, and the participants headed home, the Nazi persecution of the Jews resumed vigorously. In the summer of 1936, Jews were no longer considered German citizens, and half the Jewish population was excluded from numerous lines of work.

Young Klaus knew his days in Germany were numbered.

The Calm Before the Storm

When Klaus Ulrich Landsberg was born on July 7, 1916, Adolf Hitler was a twenty-five-year-old orderly in the Bavarian army. By the time Klaus reached eight, Hitler was leading the National

Socialist party and attacking both the Treaty of Versailles and the Jews. The organization of Storm Troopers he formed now numbered ten-thousand members.

Meanwhile, Hitler's fascination with the propaganda possibilities of television had created a favorable climate for the new medium's development, and for some time the Nazi leader even tolerated a predominance of Jewish scientists working in the fledgling industry.

Peter and Klaus as children

Born into a well-to-do Berlin family, Klaus and his older brother Peter grew up in a privileged environment. His father, Franz, was a lawyer and a judge, and his mother, Kathe, was the daughter of a wealthy German banker.

In Peter Landsberg's words: "We had a comfortable and happy family life. Our home in the Berlin suburb of Nikolassee was always a center of animated reunions with friends and families with whom we shared skiing and sailing vacations.

As children, Klaus and I enjoyed playing soccer, climbing trees and doing somersaults on the beautiful green meadow that stretched beyond our house to the edge of a lake."

Their father was a serious, disciplined man. He instilled in both sons a strong sense of duty and accountability. I found him to be a kind and patient man, who throughout Klaus's career advised him on all legal matters. His mother Kathe was a sweet, elegant lady, totally dedicated to her family and deeply interested in the arts. We became great friends.

As a young couple, Franz and Kathe were followers of the

Franz and Kathe Landsberg, parents of Peter and Klaus

Bauhaus movement, then flourishing among Berlin's young intelligentsia. They described themselves as agnostics. I once asked my father-in-law what that meant. "We defer judgment on matters for which there is insufficient evidence. That includes religion," he said, "but it does not make us any less proud of our Jewish heritage."

The senior Landsberg traced his family roots to his great-great grandfather Bzallael who lived in the town of Landsberg in Upper

Silesia, a hamlet, owned by a long succession of German dukedoms. In 1810, with the emancipation of the Jewish people in Western Europe, Bzallael adopted the name Landsberg for his family, and with their newfound rights, succeeding generations of Landsbergs produced a crop of honored and accomplished citizens. They made valuable contributions to science, politics, art and literature as physicians, judges, geologists, archeologists, chemists, professors and statesmen.

Otto Landsberg, a grandson of Bzallael and cousin to Franz, helped negotiate the Treaty of Versailles for Germany in 1919, was a member of the first German government, served as its Minister of Justice and as German Ambassador to Belgium.

Both Klaus and Peter would also pursue their goals.

Peter and I became regular pen pals after Klaus died in 1956, mostly because he relied on me for news of his parents.

"My dream was to become an agronomist and to help create a "green" nation where Jews could live in peace," Peter revealed.

"Klaus passionately embraced technology as a means of benefitting humanity. He was six years younger than I was, and as teenagers, we had little in common. As adults, we remained distant. After I left Germany in 1931, we only saw each other once, when I visited him in Prague, where he was studying."

In the early 1980s, Peter wrote that he had just been to Germany at the invitation of the government of West Berlin, after being away from his native country for fifty-one years. The invitation was extended to everyone born in Berlin who left because of the Nazi regime. Thirty thousand refugees from around the world accepted the goodwill gesture. Many did not.

My desire to revisit the places where I lived during my boyhood years was so strong. I accepted the invitation, with no regrets. We were treated royally. They paid for the flight, accommodations at the best hotels, receptions, theater performances and gave each person a daily stipend of thirty marks.

During my stay, I took a train to Nikolassee, the town where Klaus and I grew up. Nothing had changed. Nikolassee remained a suburb of villas, not affected by destruction during the war. I was so excited to see the old town hall and the school where Klaus and I studied as young boys. I remembered the day our principal was dismissed when he refused to fly the Swastika over the school.

I stood for a while in front of our home on Gerkratstrasse, and after walking uphill to the three-story structure my father built in 1913, I took a deep breath and knocked on the door.

An older man answered, and when I told him who I was, he embraced me warmly. He and his wife invited me in for coffee and a tour of the house. Except for the furnishings that were no longer there, the windows, the doors, the floor tiles in the kitchen, the parquetry floors in the dining and living rooms, and in Vati's library, were just as I remembered them.

Passing through each of the rooms brought back fond memories. The lake beyond the meadow is where my parents kept our large sailboat named Cobra. On weekends, our family sailed toward Potsdam where friends had a home by the water and where we played croquet on their lawn and went swimming and dancing. It was the quiet time before the storm that would eventually send us all in different directions."

Unlike his brother, Klaus spoke very little about his youth in Germany. He resented having his family and others robbed of their freedom and their possessions. Most of all, I think he resented the discrimination – the injustice of it all—and the fact that so many died in Hitler's Holocaust.

His mother once told me she suspected Klaus had developed a "micro-complex" when trying to explain to me why her son needed to work so hard. He needed to prove himself. I never discussed that issue with him. Klaus willingly spoke about the natural beauty of the landscape where he lived as a child; how he loved technology and sports, and how much he enjoyed sailing on the lake by his house. He missed his beloved companions—a black German shepherd named Assi and a white one named Ino. Both boys also fondly remembered their pet goats, Bianca, and Schwartze, that kept the family well supplied with goat milk and cheese during World War I when their father was sent to the Eastern front to fight the Russians.

Klaus also mentioned Irmchen, his teenage girlfriend, and others he'd known. He frequently spoke of their live-in tutor Onklechen (Little Uncle), whom the parents hired to remedy their sons' poor grades in school. Both boys were very fond of their youthful multi-talented, science-minded mentor who also played several instruments. Klaus dabbled at the piano and became proficient at the accordion.

The Young Experimenter

As fascinated as Klaus was with music and sports, during the thirteen years that I knew him, he never found time to indulge in either activity. Nothing intrigued him more than the incipient world of electronics.

When he was just six years old, he emptied a box of matches, and inside he built a simple crystal radio receiver. Growing up, he would rebuild and refine his radios, and by the time he was eleven, he could tune in to the radio broadcasts that were starting to fill the airwaves all across Europe, on equipment he designed and built himself.

For mother Kathe, it was a bit overwhelming. He often stayed up late tinkering with his radio receiver, causing his mother to scold him about bedtime. "Klauschen!" she would shout, "Turn off that radio, and go to sleep. You have school in the morning."

"Yes, Mutti," he would reply. He had hollowed out a small space in the wall beside his bed, inserted his radio inside, and covered it with matching wallpaper – effectively hiding it from sight, but not from the sound. Through a small opening, he could plug in his homemade headphones and tune-in on the world. At sixteen, he submitted and won first prize for his design of an all-wave radio receiver—the most powerful at that time and the only noncommercial apparatus exhibited at a Berlin Radio Exhibition.

Klaus also told me how much he enjoyed listening to the musical broadcasts from the Cathedral of Notre Dame. The Gregorian chants gave him "a feeling of serenity and permanence," that did not exist for Jews in Germany in the early 1930s. These broadcasts were his introduction to Catholicism; a religion Klaus would later embrace.

As his boys grew older, Franz encouraged them to become not only better thinkers but also good craftsmen. He believed in the Bauhaus notion, that instead of designing a metal sculpture and then sending the design off to a welder the artist should be the craftsman, or in this case, also the welder.

During school vacations, Vati sent Klaus to Amsterdam, to a cousin's factory that specialized in the design and manufacture of precision electrical components. He was grateful to his father for that hands-on experience, which ranged from shoveling coal into the furnaces that melted the ore to creating the steel tools. During World War II, when faced with a shortage of electronic parts, Klaus knew how to build what he needed for his work.

As a youngster, Klaus showed a strong desire to pursue his artistic inclination and appeared in many plays. In his early teens, he took courses for aspiring young actors conducted by the famous director Max Rheinhardt. What he learned about lighting and stagecraft techniques would later help him in programming for television.

By his late teens, he thoroughly understood the process of electronic transmission and built the equipment to put his theories to practical use. He obtained his EE (electrical engineer) and CE (communications engineer) degrees at the Czech Technical University in Prague.

While also lecturing and giving television demonstrations, Klaus took some postgraduate courses in engineering at the University of Berlin, although after 1933, Jews were not allowed to study at German universities. Presumably, he was given certain privileges at that time as one of the engineers assigned to the 1936 Olympic Games.

Following the Olympics, Klaus worked as a development engineer in the laboratory of Dr. Arthur Korn, a former professor at the University of Berlin who was dismissed due to his Jewish ancestry.

Dr. Korn was one of the foremost experts in the field of visual transmissions in the 1930s. He developed the first successful means of sending pictures by wire – a system that would eventually become a feature of virtually every newsroom in the world. For decades, the Associated Press "wire photo" and the United Press "telephoto," were the means by which news pictures were received by newspapers, and later by television stations.

One of Dr. Korn's inventions was a device to send weather maps and military sketches to airplanes in flight. Its military applications were quickly evident to both Hitler and Italian Prime Minister Benito Mussolini and were put to use during the Spanish Civil War.

The idea of transmitting electronic information to airplanes was intriguing to Klaus, and he was soon working on an idea of his own, a guidance system to help pilots land in poor visibility.

Klaus considered submitting the plans for his device to the German patent office but soon realized that his invention could be the key to navigating his way out of Nazi Germany.

***

The S.S. Volendam brought Klaus to New York on October 13, 1937

CHAPTER 3

Passport to Freedom

Klaus and his family had begun to dread what was going on in Germany. All the words of goodwill from the Berlin Olympics were forgotten as the Nazis prepared for war. The anti-Semitic furor was being stoked daily by Hitler's propaganda machine. Every week brought a new set of rules and regulations designed to make life uncomfortable for Jews, as the Nazi regime encouraged them to leave.

By 1937 and 1938, the Nazi government had established its practice of Aryanization (*Arisierung*) which meant "to make Aryan." Hitler was consumed with his vision of a racially pure master race that had a duty to control the world. This obsession focused on the forced expulsion of so-called "non-Aryans," mainly Jews, from Nazi Germany and its territories.

The process started by depriving its victims of their wealth and ended with the Holocaust when it finally deprived them of their remaining property and their lives. It entailed the transfer of Jewish property into "Aryan" hands to "de-Jew the German economy." It forced Jewish owners to sell their businesses at bargain prices and forbade Jewish doctors from treating non-Jews, and Jewish lawyers from practicing law. Eventually, after Klaus's parents joined him in

America, his father, a noted jurist, dedicated himself to helping Jewish families in their quest for restitution of confiscated property.

Early on, Klaus had his sights set on going to America, but how would he overcome the bureaucratic hurdles to get there? Immigration applicants had to provide affidavits from multiple sponsors, and a waiting number within a quota established for their country of birth. This severely limited their chances to emigrate.

As it turned out, Klaus had a trump card to trade – what I like to call his *passport to freedom.*

Earlier, while various nations were experimenting with instrument landing systems to enable airplanes to land safely in poor weather, Klaus had an idea to advance this technology, using precision radio beams to make blind landings a reality. He had put it in writing and made diagrams of how a plane would follow the beam straight down to the runway. He was now ready to apply for a patent for his system.

After an astute clerk at the Reich Patent Office viewed the preliminary sketches that Klaus brought in and recognized their military potential, it suddenly dawned on Klaus that they wanted his landing system for Hitler's war machine. It would enable the bombers of the German *Luftwaffe* to fly in even the poorest weather, destroying targets throughout Europe, come rain or shine. The German officials told Klaus to return to the patent office within a week, with a complete set of diagrams and detailed specifications.

Klaus reasoned that if the Nazis were impressed with his landing system, perhaps the Americans might also show enough interest to put his visa request on a fast track. He now faced an agonizing decision: either remain in his homeland and deal with the consequences or get his device and himself to America. His parents encouraged him to get out of Germany.

Klaus never told me exactly how he pulled it off with the U.S. Embassy in Berlin, but they did give him one of the coveted visas without the usual wait. He always made light of his escape from Germany, but he must have had plenty of harrowing moments—the hurried packing, concerns about leaving his family behind, and riding the night train out of Berlin to Holland.

Fortunately, for Klaus, he had worked at an electronics factory in Holland and could pass as a German employee of the Dutch company with letters he had from the bosses there. Still, there were those tense moments as the train approached the border between Germany and Holland, and it was time to present his papers. They were in order, and he could leave Germany.

Arriving in Rotterdam, Holland, Klaus boarded the *S.S. Volendam* of the Holland America line for the trip across the North Atlantic. He told me that for more than a week, the winds of the Atlantic Ocean played havoc, whipping giant waves into foamy crests and sending woozy passengers below deck. But for him, on this first transatlantic crossing, nothing could have dampened his spirits except for having left his elderly parents behind to face an uncertain future in Nazi Germany.

The fog was rolling in as the ship slid into New York Harbor on October 13, 1937. The harbor was teeming with vessels of all sizes and showing off its centerpiece—the Lady of Liberty—enveloped by a thin veil of mist. Like millions of immigrants who had come before, Klaus experienced that gripping emotional moment on seeing the legendary beacon of hope welcoming him.

At that instant, he said, he impulsively made a dash to his cabin, gathered several letters of recommendation, keeping the one from his mentor Dr. Korn, and tossing the others overboard. He wanted to believe that in this land of opportunity, all he would need to succeed was passion, hard work, and perseverance. He wanted to make it in America, on his own.

For this newcomer, America's best attributes were centered in the lively, pulsating city of New York—in its diversity, its culture, its style, and its energy. Before long the Empire State and Chrysler buildings, Rockefeller Center, Times Square, the Bronx Zoo, the Brooklyn Bridge, had all become as familiar to the young German as Berlin's *Reichstag,* the *Tiergarten* and the meadow where he played as a child.

Sharp Minds

That letter of recommendation from Dr.Korn, largely based on Klaus's achievements as a development engineer, resulted in an offer from Philo T. Farnsworth to be part of the engineering team at the Farnsworth Laboratories in Philadelphia.

Farnsworth chose new workers carefully. Acceptance to his "lab gang" was predicated on an applicant's willingness to take chances, and find a way of doing the assignment at hand.

"I am building men, not gadgets," Farnsworth once said of his unique leadership style. It was that thinking that Klaus would later adopt for himself in assembling his close-knit "dream team."

In reading about Farnsworth, I was intrigued by similarities I found between the two men, in spite of their different backgrounds. While Farnsworth was the Utah-born product of a Mormon farming family, and Klaus was a Berlin-born product of an affluent middle-class Jewish family, both had a similar amazing grasp of scientific subjects, even as youngsters.

Klaus was ten years younger than Farnsworth, but no doubt aware of the inventive American genius through Farnsworth's many visits to Germany and the partnership between German electronics manufacturers and Farnsworth's company during the launch of television at the Berlin Olympics.

Both astonished their science teachers at a very young age. Farnsworth was twenty-two when he conceived the principle of an all-electronic TV system that was the basis for what is in use in television today. Klaus was sixteen in 1932 when he won first prize for creating the most powerful all-wave radio receiver known at that time. Their curiosity about technical matters, their approach to how things could work, was boundless, as was their vision.

Both men dabbled at the piano, and both had one favorite instrument. Farnsworth played the violin proficiently, and Klaus played the accordion just as well. When Lawrence Welk was brought into television, Klaus surprised him by playing *Ach Du Lieber Augustin* on Welk's accordion, amazing the bandleader as much as it did me.

Farnsworth had been embroiled in a lengthy legal battle with RCA over who owned the patent rights to electronic television. Finally, in 1939, RCA backed down and paid Farnsworth $1 million to license his inventions. RCA was eager to become the dominant player in television and wanted to get rid of this obstacle.

The World of Tomorrow

That same year, Klaus was back in New York, lured by an offer from RCA and its NBC television subsidiary to participate in presenting the first public television demonstration at the 1939 New York World's Fair, while also working as an independent consulting engineer.

The theme for the fair was "The World of Tomorrow, " and RCA saw it as a golden opportunity to capitalize on people's curiosity about television and lend historical significance to the launch of the new medium. Ten days before the opening of the fair, RCA president David Sarnoff dedicated his company's pavilion in a flowery fashion: "It is with a feeling of humbleness that I come to this moment of announcing the birth in this country of a new art so important in its implications that it is bound to affect all society. It is an art which shines like a torch of hope in a troubled world."

An RCA ad at the time sounded like a birth announcement from a proud parent: "In initiating the first regular American television programs at this time, RCA believes that it is contributing to the growth of a lusty infant whose future is likely to be brilliant." The inaugural broadcast also carried the prestige of Franklin Delano Roosevelt's presence, marking the first time a US president had ever appeared on television and offering a parting look at a vanishing pre-war world.

Klaus had the perfect résumé to be on the TV crew at the World's Fair. After all, his Olympic experience in Berlin made him one of the world's few television engineers who, at that time, had worked on a remote broadcast of a huge special event.

The fair, opening on April 30, 1939, was televised to a large audience on the fairgrounds and a handful of TV sets in the New York area. A signal was sent from a mobile television van to the Empire State Building transmitter and rebroadcast to the television sets at the fair. *The New York Times* described it this way: "Reports from receiving outposts scattered throughout a 50-mile radius of New York indicated that the spectacle by television was highly successful and that a new industry had been launched into the World of Tomorrow. It was estimated that from 100 to 200 receivers were in tune and that possibly 1,000 persons looked in on the pageant brightened on the screens by a sun described by the cameramen as ideal for telecasting."

Some 45 million people attended the New York World's Fair, and many spectators were eager to look at the new gadget that could send moving pictures into people's homes. One big attraction was the chance for fairgoers to see themselves on TV for the first time. RCA had a spot where they could stand in front of a camera and view their electronic image on a receiver. I don't know how many of them waved at the camera and yelled, "Hi, Mom!"

RCA was joined by GE, Westinghouse and other TV-set manufacturers in showing off the new medium. *Broadcasting* magazine, a trade publication, said the companies were "totally unprepared for the crowds that have engulfed the exhibits of this new broadcasting art."

While there was much interest in TV, few people plunked down hard-earned cash for those first sets. It was, after all, the tail end of the Great Depression and TV's were selling for $200 to $1,000 at a time when you could buy a brand-new Ford V8 for $850.

Having participated in the launch of TV at the fair, Klaus soon found himself a tiny apartment, and being a passionate sailor, acquired a small sailboat and spent most weekends on the Hudson River. By then, his parents had left Germany with only household goods and were living in England. Soon after, they were able to join Klaus in New York.

The story of what happened to Klaus's invention to enable blind landings by airplanes gets a little murky at this point. Klaus said he applied for a patent, but the rights may have been scooped up by his employer, RCA. Government records show that RCA was active in patenting navigational aids for aircraft from 1937 to 1940.

Meanwhile, inventor Allen B. Dumont had become aware of Klaus's qualifications at RCA and offered to sign him on as television design and development engineer for the New York Dumont Laboratories, a pioneer television organization. He was called on to supervise the technical operations of the television unit at US Army maneuvers in Canton, New York, set up Dumont's experimental New York statio W2XVW, and assist with the production of that station's first TV shows.

During his time at Dumont, Klaus invented a high sensitivity television camera pickup tube that was quickly snapped up by the military as a possible surveillance tool. It was promptly declared a military secret. Klaus Landsberg had joined the ranks of inventors whose many contributions to the war effort would remain unheralded.

Paramount Pictures, a major stockholder in the Dumont Laboratories, also had an eye on the young engineer. Earlier, at the time of the opening of the World's Fair, Paramount president Barney Balaban had announced that the studio's new $12 million facilities in Hollywood would be equipped with television.

And, as those plans moved along, Paramount courted Klaus to make them a reality.

***

CHAPTER 4

Go West Young Man

Horace Greeley's familiar call, "Go west, young man," did not go unheeded by twenty-five-year-old Klaus Landsberg when in 1941 he jumped at the chance to head for the Golden West and grow with the country. With only two suitcases, parts of two iconoscope cameras, and the blind trust of his new employer, Paramount Pictures, Klaus boarded the train to Hollywood.

The Super Chief

Riding the *Super Chief*, the flagship of the Atchison, Topeka and Santa Fe Railway, resplendent in its striking warbonnet colors, would be an adventure in itself. Its passengers included celebrities, headliners and movie moguls who regularly used the train on roundtrips between the East and West coasts. So, for the next three days aboard the "Train of the Stars", Klaus enjoyed luxury porter service, superb meals, and Pullman facilities.

One can't help but wonder what his thoughts were as he sped across the 2,227 miles to Los Angeles, viewing for the first time the "amber waves of grain" of America's expansive heartland while hoping someday to see television stretch from "sea to shining sea."

Klaus was headed into unchartered waters, charged with singlehandedly setting up an experimental television station. He couldn't have been more eager to face this most demanding challenge of his life, but he was also prepared to face skepticism and opposition to his efforts in Hollywood.

For movie theater owners, the new medium was an unwelcome intruder that threatened to affect their attendance. Other stumbling blocks had to do with the wartime scarcity of components he would need to build what he hoped would be the most powerful TV transmitter in existence anywhere. Klaus never lacked in confidence or determination. The word "cannot" simply did not exist in his vocabulary.

On that bright sunny day, after pulling in at Los Angeles's luxurious Union Station, the last of the great railway stations built in the United States, Klaus began to feel the uniqueness of the city that proudly flaunted its Spanish heritage, and bore the grandiose name of *Nuestra Señora La Reina de Los Angeles.* The station's splendid lobby, with its marble floors, colorful handmade tiles, and shady arcades was filled with starry-eyed newcomers nursing hopes of making it big in movies, as well as countless servicemen also milling about, many destined to combat duty in the approaching war with Japan.

Klaus was exempted from serving in the military as the U.S. Government considered the advancement of television technology a potentially important tool in its defense arsenal. Already, work was underway on TV-guided drone warplanes and other military applications for the new medium.

With his electronic equipment safely in hand, Klaus hailed a cab.

"Where to?" said the driver, a heavyset man with a Russian accent.

"Paramount Studios."

"You actor?"

"I'm an engineer."

"I'm 'extra,' but I drive cabs between gigs. Done a few Westerns at Paramount and RKO," he rambled on. "Mostly I'd sit at a bar, and get punched in the jaw."

Meanwhile, Klaus was more absorbed with the landscape. He had never seen so many slender palm trees silhouetted against the sky.

In 1832, when Richard Dana, author of *Two Years Before the Mast*, first visited Los Angeles, it was a sleepy *pueblo* with one thousand people.

By 1885, a railroad was in place that provided a direct connection with the East and Los Angeles experienced a rapid gain in population, trade, and commerce—notably the spectacular rise and growth of the motion-picture industry, a key player in the region's development.

As Los Angeles grew, so did its satellite cities, a loose confederation of neighboring towns, each having its lifestyle, so that Los Angeles became known as a string of suburbs looking to become a major city. Pasadena, with its conservative old families and its annual Tournament of Roses, was a world apart from Beverly Hills, with its curving tree-lined streets, bridle paths, and movie-star mansions. The distant hills surrounding the citrus groves of Pomona attracted some newcomers; others working for Douglas Aircraft built their homes by the cliffs of Santa Monica. Many drifted toward Huntington Park, the center of the middle-class residential section, or to San Pedro and Wilmington, industrial districts close to their jobs. Angelenos in the 1940s already had more cars per capita than other Americans and drove incredible distances just to get to work, take in a movie, or simply visit friends.

From the start, Klaus knew the key to establishing a foothold for Paramount's experimental TV station in Los Angeles was to latch onto the city's ethnic diversity.

Los Angeles proper was the nation's largest city in an area of 451 square miles, and Greater Los Angeles covered almost ten times that much.

It had close to one-quarter of a million citizens of Mexican descent, who were proud of their dual heritage. The black population, attracted by good jobs in the defense industry, had increased and became more vocal about their issues, and Klaus felt strongly that television could help all Angelenos improve relations with other races. This was true of the five thousand Chinese and thirty-six thousand Japanese residents of Los Angeles County at that time.

More and more Midwestern families were migrating to California, and in the immediate post-war period, returning war veterans chose to settle in this booming land of opportunity. It was blessed with a fabulous climate and the absence of hidebound social conventions.

Now, seventy-some years later, immigrant enclaves exist throughout Los Angeles, labeled as Little Tokyo. Little Armenia, Little Korea, and so forth, and the English spoken here is a language cocktail—a mixture of regional dialects contributing to a new homogenized speech referred to by linguists as "California English." Klaus hadn't expected a welcoming committee as he crossed the threshold into Paramount's "dream factory," but neither did he expect to feel expendable. His New York boss Paul Raibourn, president of Paramount Television Productions, had sent him off with a pat on the back, and all he said was: "I'm counting on you, Klaus.

After being cleared at the main gate of the studios, he was handed a cart for his two suitcases, and found his way to the executive offices through a labyrinth of sound stages and sets, teeming with actors coming and going. A production manager greeted him, saying,

The Bronson Ave. gate at Paramount Pictures

"You must be the guy they sent out here from New York to set up some kind of experimental station. We've arranged for you to stay at the Hayward apartments 'til we get you settled."

"Could I see the space I'll be working in ?"

"Sure, sure."

These were the days of cinematic masterpieces -- *the Maltese Falcon* with Humphrey Bogart; Orson Welles's *Citizen Kane*, a movie milestone; *How Green Was My Valley*, with Maureen O'Hara and Walter Pidgeon; *The Little Foxes,* with Bette Davis; *Sergeant York* with Gary Cooper; the classic *Casablanca,* with Humphrey Bogart and Ingrid Bergman; *Mrs. Minniver,* the wartime epic with Greer Garson. The competition among the studios was fierce.

"We're putting out some forty films this year," said the production manager. "I'm afraid we don't have much space to offer you, Klaus. How much equipment have you got coming in?"

"It's all right here, in these suitcases," Klaus said. "Just two iconoscope cameras. The rest I'll build myself."

"Hell, then I guess you can manage with half of a sound stage."

" It'll do fine."

The Competition

Klaus was not the first television pioneer to work in Los Angeles. In 1930, Don Lee, an LA Cadillac dealer, and owner of two California radio stations thought the idea of sending pictures through the airwaves could be a huge moneymaker. Lee hired Harry Lubcke, a promising twenty-four-year-old engineer with a degree from the University of California at Berkeley and gave him the title, Director of Television of the Don Lee Broadcasting System.

Their first TV studio was located in downtown Los Angeles at the corner of 7th and Bixel Streets where the first broadcast took place on May 10, 1931. Lubcke and his team sent an image from one side of a room to the other. The equipment was homemade and clunky; the pictures were fuzzy and crude. However, the experiment showed enough promise, which the following month the Federal Government granted the Don Lee Broadcasting System an experimental television license: W6XAO.

The station took to the air two days before Christmas in 1931 and would soon rack up some "firsts." In 1932, Lubcke and his staff placed a television receiver aboard a passenger plane and transmitted images from the ground to a group of press representatives as they flew over Los Angeles.

On March 10, 1933, a magnitude 6.4 earthquake struck Long Beach, California, killing 120 people. W6XAO arranged for newsreel film of the disaster to be processed rapidly and rushed to the station. Within hours, images of the earthquake damage were on the air, demonstrating television's potential for news reporting. Also in March, W6XAO was the first station to televise a full-length motion picture, *The Crooked Circle,* that was still running in theaters. The studio saw no harm in lending the movie to the TV station, since there were so few receivers in Los Angeles at the time. Besides, it was great publicity.

Lubcke's early television transmissions relied on a mechanical system for sending the TV picture—whirling discs perforated with tiny holes that would scan a beam of light across a frame of film with a light-sensing photoelectric cell picking up the changes in intensity as the beam passed through light and dark areas in the picture.

I still remember Klaus trying to explain that concept to me, by shining a flashlight on a wall and moving the spot of light rapidly back and forth. "You see, it looks like a line of light," he said as he swung the flashlight. "Now imagine placing a line of light on top of another, on top of another. Soon, you have filled a whole frame. But it has to be done over and over, many times per second."

Lubcke's first experiments were limited to eighty lines of resolution for each frame transmitted because those early mechanical systems were not capable of scanning faster or more finely. The engineers knew that the holy grail of television design was an *all-electronic* system with no moving parts.

In the course of gathering personal memories of those pioneering years, I had the pleasure of a visit from Harry Lubcke after I contacted him for an interview. I had no idea we were neighbors. He lived on the hill just above me and walked down to my house.

I asked him how well he had known Klaus and what his opinion of him was.

"Klaus was a tough competitor," he said.

"He thought highly of you," I remarked.

"It was mutual," he said.

Among papers left by Klaus's father, I found a letter Lubcke sent to Klaus, who had just undergone the first of his seven cancer operations.

"I called the hospital," wrote Lubcke, "and was glad to hear you had left and, therefore, must be on the mend. I have thought of you often in relation to your difficulty and extend my very best wishes and hopes for your speedy recovery. Keep a stiff upper lip, Klaus, believe in yourself and in that greater power above that will always help us."

Coincidentally, Philo T. Farnsworth, for whom both Lubcke and Klaus worked as development engineers, once lived on New Hampshire Avenue in the 1920s, only blocks from where I now live. It was where he began tinkering with electronic components on the dining room table of the apartment he shared with his bride "Pem."

(Elma). At that time, he attracted the interest of well-heeled investors in the San Francisco area and left Hollywood to set up shop there.

By 1928, Farnsworth had demonstrated his new electronic device for transmitting pictures, the "Image Dissector." Sensing the profit potential in television, Farnsworth and associates used a dollar sign as the first image they would transmit.

California, the place that spawned a great gold rush in 1849, was once again proving itself a place for fortune-seeking and invention.

***

CHAPTER 5

Performing Without a Net

Klaus's mandate was to set up shop in Hollywood and try to figure out what the new medium could do. He was now in charge of Paramount's Los Angeles station, W6XYZ, one of only six US television stations that remained on the air during the war years.

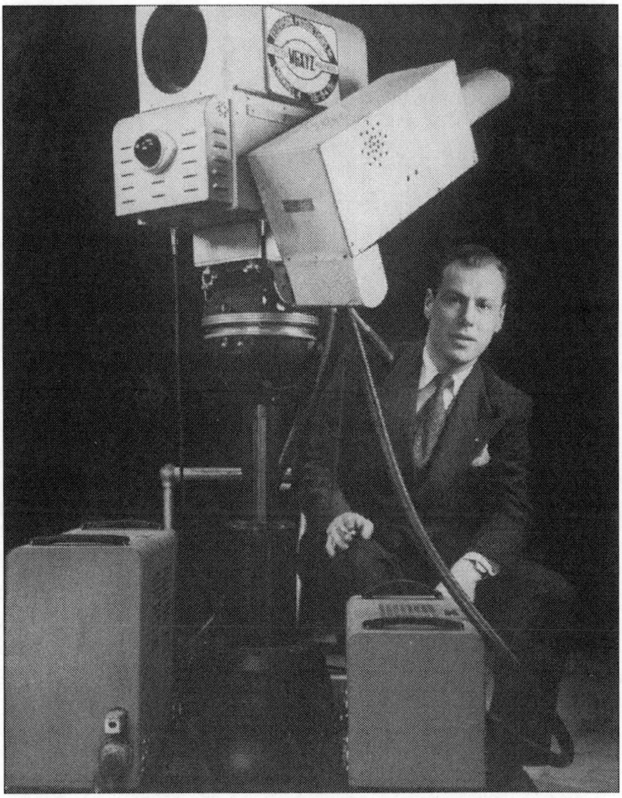

Klaus and early Iconoscope camera

As soon as Klaus assembled enough parts to set up his transmitter, the station was on the air, signing on for the first time in September of 1942. He began sizing up who would be out there watching. In those days, TV set owners numbered about three hundred and were usually radio buffs who built their sets. Klaus wanted to reach out to them and garner their support.

He always said his audiences were the most important element of his work. He wanted to virtually hug his Los Angeles viewers and create a bond with them. He needed them to gauge the likes and dislikes of his audience, and soon gathered a slew of supporters.

I remember being one of the poll takers. Once or twice a week, I was given a list of set owners to call for their reaction to the picture quality on their TV screens that day. Klaus then used their comments to adjust the transmitter or program content.

I'd ask them, "Is the Indian in a good mood tonight?" The Indian-head test pattern was introduced by RCA in 1939 and became a TV icon in the 1940s. It was broadcast during a station's downtime after a show ended.

Shortly after station W6XYZ took to the air in 1942, Klaus broadcast his first "remote," although it wasn't terribly far from his studio. From another corner of the Paramount lot, his cameras went to the set of the movie *This Gun for Hire,* a film *noir* starring Alan Ladd and Veronica Lake. It was the breakthrough role for Ladd, who became a major star in the 1940s and 50s and starred with Miss Lake in several movies.

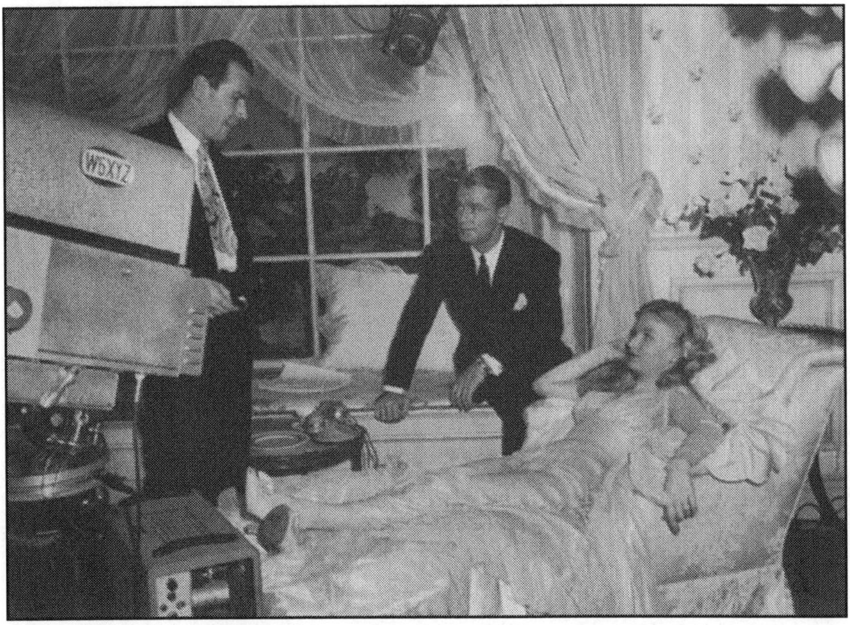

Klaus with Alan Ladd and Veronica Lake

Klaus kept his cameras on the go, fielding a mobile unit in 1943 to broadcast local events such as the Sheriff's Rodeo from the Los Angeles Coliseum. Since experimental TV stations were not permitted by the FCC to sell commercial airtime, the cost of keeping the station on the air was borne entirely by Paramount. In 1943, the budget came to $896,000, including $300,000 for employee salaries and $576,000 for programing costs.

In 1944, Paramount continued using the station to plug its movies. When noted writer-director Preston Sturges completed his screwball comedy *The Miracle of Morgan's Creek,* he went on W6XYZ to give audiences a 30-minute preview. Using still pictures, he narrated a summary of the movie without giving away what the "miracle" was.

Variety summed it up this way: "Picture came through well on the receiver and augured well for that day when studios and television work hand in hand."

The plot of the movie was rather racy for the times—Betty Hutton playing a small-town girl who attends a wild send-off party for the troops and wakes up the next morning to discover that she is married to somebody she can't remember. In due time, she also finds out that she's pregnant. Rated "B" and panned as morally objectionable by the Catholic Legion of Decency, the picture was nonetheless a huge hit and played to standing-room-only audiences. Many critics regard it as one of the greatest movie comedies of all times.

On a more serious level, many of W6XYZ's programs were designed to help the war effort and satisfy the station's "public interest" obligation as laid out by the Federal Communications Commission. In its October 1943 edition, the magazine *Popular Mechanics* described some of those programs: "This television station at present devotes its regular bi-weekly broadcasts to civilian defense subjects. It radiates sight-and-sound demonstrations on how to seal your home against poison gas, how to extinguish incendiary bombs, and tips for air raid wardens. Experts in first aid show how injured people should be cared for, and once a week an instructor in Judo and self-defense gives a complete lesson on some aspect of personal protection."

Among the viewers were officers of the Los Angeles Police Department watching at sub-stations where receivers were set up to carry the instructional programming.

Another regular feature was a program called *Hits and Bits.* It was a potpourri of whatever Klaus and his staff could come up with to fill the airtime—a show that ran the gamut from celebrity interviews to exhibitions of wrestling in the studio.

To serve as host, Klaus picked character actor Dick Lane, described as "courtly, blue-eyed and broad-shouldered." Dick had a rather eclectic resume, breaking into entertainment with a medicine show after running away from home, hawking Kickapoo Indian Elixir, Salve & Soap. Later, he toured Europe with a traveling circus, performing an "iron jaw" routine that required him to hang by his teeth from a spinning bar suspended at the top of the tent. In the movies, he gained a measure of fame as Inspector Faraday opposite Chester Morris in the *Boston Blackie* series of whodunit films. Dick would appear in 256 pictures. He and Klaus hit it off when Dick stopped by the TV studio one day in 1942.

"I went in, and there was just one guy, who I later found out was Klaus Landsberg," Lane said. "We liked each other and worked together after a day's filming, experimenting with scripted shows, audience participation shows, and quizzes—trying to see what the public would like."

Klaus saw from the beginning that Dick Lane had a gift for gab and by 1943, Dick was a regular on the station, the first member of Klaus's repertory company.

That was the nature of television in Los Angeles in the early years. Show after show; all were locally produced "live." Filmed programing was scarce; videotape wouldn't be invented until the mid-'50's, and there were no network connections to New York. If there were mistakes, if somebody forgot his or her lines, if the props failed to work properly, viewers got to see the slip-ups in all their glory. Klaus and his troupe of players were, in more ways than one, performing without a net. However, they were getting plenty of accolades for this experiment.

The *Hollywood Reporter* wrote, "Technically, Klaus Landsberg's efforts are well received. That he knows the technical end of television, no one can deny. In his laboratory at Paramount, he is laying the foundation for many new and much-needed improvements in the field of video. As a production man, he is hard to beat and ranks high in our estimation as a man who knows what entertainment means."

Primping for TV

Klaus recruited me for one of the shows, and I got some firsthand experience on what it took to be a live television performer in the early 1940's.

Back then, makeup that looked good in real life or that worked on film, sometimes had a ghastly appearance on black-and-white TV. The Iconoscope camera tubes in use then gave performers a pasty-faced appearance when they wore regular makeup.

Hollywood's famous Max Factor and his son began working on darker shades of their "pancake" makeup that produced good results with the early electronic cameras. Never mind that people wearing it looked zombie-like in real life. Women had to apply green lipstick and rouge because the color red had a very pale appearance when televised.

The garish makeup used in early TV

Blondes were not having more fun on television in those days. The technicians coined a term, "blizzard head" to describe a female television performer having hair so blond as to require special lighting to prevent a flare or halo from appearing in place of her hair. And, banks of photoflood lamps generating brutal amounts of heat, were perched uncomfortably close to the performers.

On that early interview show, Klaus asked me and Erico Verissimo, a noted Brazilian author, and visiting scholar, to be part of a discussion on South American issues. After all, Carmen Miranda was a big deal at the movies, and Klaus figured people would be interested in the goings-on in the southern hemisphere.

Verissimo's first experience with television makeup and lighting was traumatic and he later described it hilariously in his popular book *The Return of the Black Cat.* I translated this excerpt from the original Portuguese version:

<u>June 5th</u>. A washroom at Paramount Studios at 7:30 p.m.

Using a Gillette blade I carried in my pocket, I shave myself before a mirror because, under the merciless lights of television, the slightest vestige of a beard will create a frightening image of me. As the blade slides over my face, I think that after all, I have done a little of everything in the last two years in the United States. However, I never expected to be in this place, in these circumstances, about to have my image transformed into electrical impulses and projected with the speed of light through space and put back together again...where?...by whom? And for what? That is a question I've rarely asked myself because it takes the spontaneity out of life.

The television studio is on one of the "sets" at Paramount. Mariana (my wife) and Evelyn's parents are in the audience. They direct me to a dressing room at the top of the stairs, and there I find myself in the company of a semi-nude ballerina, an oldish woman who tames canaries, a magician in tails, and a Czechoslovakian caricaturist wearing a black velvet beret.

A somewhat effeminate guy approaches me, takes a grim look at my face and tells me, "You need a little touch of special makeup."

"Is that really necessary?" I ask.

"Oh, it's indispensable."

"All right then."

He takes a small tin of "pancake" makeup the shade of terra cotta, runs a damp sponge over it and then spreads it over my face. Next, to me the semi-clad woman (now I see that she is not a ballerina but a contortionist) is rehearsing her number; she is upside down with both supportive arms on the floor, and her legs bent over to her neck, looking like an enormous spider.

The oldster with the canaries primps before a mirror; the magician prepares the top hat from which the rabbit, seated sadly in the corner of the dressing room, will eventually emerge.

The makeup man takes a lipstick of brownish color and paints my lips.

"This too?"

"Uh, hum,"

"I'm demoralized," I mumble.

Finally, I join Evelyn. We go over the details of our dialog, which will be improvised as we examine the photos we will use in our "number."

The show begins.

The master of ceremonies, a movie comedian (Dick Lane) does the introductions. When our turn comes around, Evelyn and I are seated at a table, as two television cameras similar to motion-picture cameras move slowly toward us. We're told to watch the "green eye" on the cameras. Hanging menacingly over our heads is a microphone.

The reflectors light up. The blinding light is of such intensity that I feel the makeup on my face melting into a stream of mud that threatens to slide off my face. I have the taste of perfumed lipstick in my mouth. This is all so silly and so new.

We hear the signal. The speaker announces our appearance; the green light goes on and our images are already dashing through space. Evelyn invites me to accompany her to Brazil, and we begin looking and commenting on the photographs that are being shown in close-up while we remain invisible, and then the cameras refocus on us.

I am soaked in perspiration. The lights make me feel as if I'm in a desert at midday exposed to the most torrid and pitiless of suns. At last, our fifteen minutes are over, and our segment ends. I believe we pulled it off with ease and poise.

After the show, I walked toward my wife, still in makeup and feeling vaguely ridiculous.

"You were incredible," she said, "With that painted face you look like those bumblers of the silent movies."

Erico Verissimo had discovered that in television's pioneer days, those fifteen minutes of fame did not come easily. Although sweat-soaked and rumpled at the end, this distinguished literary figure was thrilled to take part in what he termed a "noble experiment" that would soon herald the debut of the first commercial television station west of the Mississippi.

***

Our wedding day

CHAPTER 6

Tying the Knot

On April 2, 1945, my thoughts were focused on the two most important men in my life—the one who walked me down the aisle of Blessed Sacrament Church in Hollywood, and the one standing at the altar who would soon be my husband.

As my father and I walked slowly to the beat of Wagner's "Bridal Chorus," I visualized my grandparents, uncles and aunts, cousins and friends, occupying the endless rows of empty pews. I missed sharing my happiness with them and introducing them to the man with whom I planned to spend the rest of my life.

Klaus and I had but a handful of close friends in Los Angeles. Those attending included Klaus's best man, his NBC pal George Volger; both sets of parents; and my brother Richard, who flew in from Allied military training in Kansas. The Brazilian consul and his wife served as "godparents." Others included two former Disney colleagues and the Bennison family, whom my parents befriended on a cruise. Father McCummiskey conducted the High Mass. By then, Klaus had become a Catholic.

My mother would have preferred staging this family celebration in my hometown of Rio de Janeiro, with a host of friends present, but she did it in style even without bridesmaids or ushers and only a charming little flower girl named Melissa. I wore a shimmering satin gown with an heirloom veil of Brussels lace worn by my mother at her wedding, a pair of eighteenth-century gold and pearl earrings, something blue, and a bright new penny in my shoe.

My parents later hosted a splendid brunch at the Beverly Hills Hotel, and as Klaus and I prepared to leave the hotel, an attendant rushed to tell him he was wanted on the phone. He took the call and returned with a sheepish look. "Darling, do you mind if we make a quick stop at the station? There seems to be a problem with the transmitter. I'm sure it's nothing I can't resolve in a few minutes." That day I learned the meaning of the time-honored phrase, *the show must go on.* One must never let the other players down.

It took until one a.m. before we left the station and settled into a nearby Hollywood motel for a few hours of sleep. By dawn, we were driving happily along stretches of fragrant orange orchards to our honeymoon destination, the Mission Inn in Riverside. A doting husband and the majestic images of a European castle delivered every bit of romance and enchantment I had anticipated.

I had no inkling that my marriage would be a *ménage à trois* and that television would become a demanding mistress.

Settling In

Was I ready for my new role as an American housewife? Hardly, but I had bought the American dream, lock, stock, and barrel. For young brides in postwar America, it meant having a nuclear family—husband, wife, two kids and a dog, a car and a house with a picket fence. And, of course, the wonder of wonders: a washing machine!

Looking back, it was a privilege to witness the extraordinary changes that took place in this country during World War II. Never was the motto *United We Stand, Divided We Fall* better demonstrated.

It was a time to deal with social and economic issues, a time when the people were becoming more aware of injustices that needed fixing. Labor laws changed, and blacks were given better opportunities for employment. It was also a time when women proved they could fill any male-oriented job. World War II was a turning point in the nation's history, and while it didn't remedy all evils, it revolutionized the workplace and welcomed a new era of hope and enterprise for its citizens.

We faced a huge shortage of everyday conveniences. In a letter to my parents in 1944, I wrote:

> "*We can't buy any flashlights in the States. I suggest you keep mine as a treasure. No more irons to buy, or toasters and things made of metal, not even hairpins. Everything is made of plastic. The leather is scarce, and unrationed shoes are made of cardboard. What's so wonderful about the American people, is that they wear them and don't complain.*"

Each person in a household, including babies, was allowed a book of coupons to purchase groceries and merchandise. The system was complicated, with expiration dates and color codes; red stamps to buy meats, butter, cheeses; blue stamps for frozen and canned fruits, juices, beans. Such rare items as woolen coats, silk stockings, and nylons also had their stamps. Automobiles and home appliances were no longer being made. On the other hand, fruit-and-vegetable "victory gardens" flourished, and, by the end of the war provided almost half of the produce consumed in the United States.

The military draft drained the labor force of millions of young men, so wives and girlfriends replaced them in the industrial centers to manufacture planes, ships, and ammunition. "Rosie the Riveter" became a symbol of the hard-working women participating in the war effort.

Barely a month after Klaus and I were married, we stood at the corner of Hollywood and Vine streets, crushed among a jubilant crowd, hugging total strangers as we celebrated V-E Day and the surrender of Germany on May 8, 1945. To both of us, it meant more than a victory for our side; it signified triumph over injustice and the dawn of new opportunities.

Our first home in a Hollywood bungalow

Our first home was a modest one-bedroom bungalow in a small court on Loma Linda Avenue, in a quiet back street of Hollywood. It was owned by the in-laws of Vincent Filizola, one of W6XYZ's first engineers. It was all we could afford since Klaus also maintained an apartment for his parents, where he lived before we were married.

Playing house was a novel experience for a gal raised in a household with servants, who arrived in this country with teaching credentials but minimal domestic skills. When my parents asked me what I wanted for a housewarming gift, I asked for a sewing machine and immediately enrolled in a Singer sewing course. I knew hardly anything about cooking but was eager to learn, and relied on Klaus's mother to teach me. That first year I also completed pending assignments for the State Department's Radio and Motion Picture Division.

The Rabbit Test

Early in my marriage, I wasn't sure whether a missed period or tender breasts meant anything unusual but decided to see a doctor before taking off with Klaus on a trip to San Francisco.

Modern obstetrics in the 40's provided 99 percent-accurate pregnancy results after taking the "rabbit" or the "toad" test -- unlike today, when all you do is stop at a supermarket, pick up an HPT kit, and receive your answer within two or three minutes of testing. Klaus and I were so anxious for the results that we asked my doctor to inform us by telegram, in the care of the Brazilian Consulate in San Francisco.

In those carefree days, I accompanied Klaus on most of his "scouting" jaunts, which usually meant exploring new avenues for television. On this trip to the Bay area, Klaus talked about establishing a microwave link to Northern California, and we drove up to the east peak of Mount Tamalpais, just north of San Francisco's Golden Gate – the peak clearly visible from San Francisco and the East Bay region.

Once again, line of sight was a primary consideration. "If we set up on this peak and find a couple more sites high enough along the coast, just imagine what a huge audience we'll gain," he exclaimed.

Between appointments with city officials, riding the cable car and sampling the seafood at Fisherman's Wharf, Klaus and I stopped by the Brazilian Consulate. To our delight, the awaited telegram arrived with my doctor's coded message: GOOD NEWS FROM CLEVELAND STOP ARRIVING JANUARY STOP.

Klaus was beaming and stopped at a florist to buy me a corsage. That evening we celebrated at the Top of the Mark like two giddy teens and decided if we had a son, we'd name him Cleve, choosing the doctor's clever blend of both our names.

After our son was born, Klaus hired a nurse to train me for my new role. She was a large, friendly Cherokee woman, whose clients were mostly movie stars like Lana Turner. I felt so pampered.

Klaus was in love with having a child, but he was all thumbs when it came to assisting me. One day, I asked him to change the baby.

"I'm afraid I'll stick Clevie with the safety pin!"

"You'll do fine," I assured him and watched him take the baby from his stroller, all the while admiring his gurgling son as he carefully placed him on the changing table and proceeded to remove the diaper. At that moment, it was as if someone suddenly turned on a water fountain aimed straight at Klaus's face. He looked up at me in dismay as I began to laugh uncontrollably.

"It's not funny!" he screamed and also burst out laughing. His son could do no wrong. "Just please, never ask me to do this again," he sputtered.

Little Jasper

Klaus was an early enthusiast of color television. Large teams of engineers at RCA/NBC and CBS Laboratories were working on the concept, but Klaus figured he might come up with something the big boys back East didn't have. CBS was first out of the gate with a system that was a throwback to the days of mechanical television. Dr. Peter Goldmark of CBS Labs devised a rotating wheel with red, green and blue filters that was placed between the camera lens and the pickup tube, allowing the camera to transmit the three primary colors in sequence, red-green-blue, red-green-blue.

Klaus would explain to me that at the receiving end, another color wheel spun in front of the TV screen, reproducing the red-green-blue sequence. And as the filters moved at high speed, the human eye would combine the images and see them as a color picture, all of which struck me as a bit of magic I could barely understand.

During my pregnancy, we spent long hours together after the station went off the air. Klaus used that time to develop new ideas and tinker with his transmitter, already credited with being the most powerful in existence.

I would rest on the leather couch in his office, and occasionally he would stop, light a cigarette, and reach for the coffee pot. We'd sit for a while, and he'd tell me how much he loved "working" with me, which meant he could think aloud and I would listen. He often asked me to witness his scribbled notations and diagrams with my dated signature. There was always a potential patent on his mind.

In his early experiments with color, Klaus used a film slide with the cartoon character Little Jasper. I loved little Jasper, and he soon became our secret mascot.

George Pal's "Little Jasper"

Little Jasper was created by animator and director George Pal, a Hungarian, who, like Klaus, left Europe as the Nazis were coming to power. Jasper was featured in some Technicolor cartoon shorts at Paramount for which Pal received Oscar nominations.

Using various filters in front of the tiny image, Klaus tried to find a way for that image to be transmitted in color but also receivable on regular black and white sets, something that had eluded the CBS engineers.

There was one big problem with the CBS system at that time. TV images were transmitted at 30 frames a second, and at that speed, the color filters produced an annoying flicker. CBS solved the problem by speeding the frame rate, but that meant that ordinary black and white receivers wouldn't get a viewable signal. And when CBS started experimenting with color broadcasts in Cleveland in 1951, station WEWS sent out this notice to viewers: "If you have a standard black and white television receiver, do not expect to see these special color programs. Do not imagine anything is wrong with your set when it fails to deliver a picture."

Were the broadcasters going to tell people who had just shelled out a lot of money for those new receivers, "Sorry folks, those sets are obsolete…You'll have to buy one of these new color models?"

The challenge for Klaus: figure out a way of transmitting a color TV signal that could be picked up in black and white by existing sets and wouldn't flicker as people were watching.

Klaus was thinking of applying for a patent for Little Jasper but never quite ironed out the kinks in it. Eventually, he decided that the engineering teams at CBS Labs and RCA/NBC were probably too far advanced for him to catch up.

RCA soon demonstrated an all-electronic color TV system that was compatible with existing black and white sets and didn't need any cumbersome spinning filters. It got the go-ahead from the Federal Communications Commission in 1953 and became the standard for color broadcasting. Eventually, RCA's NBC subsidiary would broadcast all its shows in "living color."

It was probably a good thing that Little Jasper was retired. George Pal had taken heat from some African-American groups because Jasper, a black character, was seen as a negative racial stereotype. The truth is neither George nor Klaus harbored any racial bias. Discriminating against blacks was the last thing on their minds.

Ebony, a magazine focusing African-Americans, printed a sympathetic article about George Pal in 1947, saying he had come from Europe in 1939 and "as a European not raised on race prejudice, he takes America for what he finds in it."

Klaus was the same way, taking America for what he found in it, and naive to the racial hang-ups of his adopted land. To him, the color of Jasper's skin mattered only as far as it could be accurately reproduced on a television screen.

Someone eventually ironed out the bugs in the color-wheel system. NASA used it in a color camera designed to survive the rigors of space travel starting with Apollo 10 in 1969. When Apollo 14 astronaut Alan Shepard played golf on the Moon in 1971, the first time the camera was used on the lunar surface, viewers all over the world got to see him in color as well as in black and white.

The Man Who Came to Dinner

Cleve must have been two when Klaus announced that his New York boss Paul Raibourn was coming to town and expressly mentioned wanting to meet me.

"I'd like to have him over for dinner," said Klaus.

"Here? In this little house?" I shuddered, "We hardly have room for a TV set."

"That's the idea," he smiled. "Paul may decide we need a larger home and give me a raise."

"I'll do my best, but I'll need Mutti's help."

Klaus's mother and I had become very close. I called her *Mutti* ("mother" in German). She was so gracious, never pushy or interfering as some mothers-in-law tend to be. I often accompanied her on bus rides to the Viktor Benes bakery and her German butcher. Each week she purchased an assortment of her family's favorite treats and kept them in a tin container that Klaus described as Mutti's Pandora box.

He adored his parents and never failed to attend his mother's weekly brunch, a ritual my son Cleve, and later my daughter Terry, still remember fondly.

Having Klaus's boss for dinner required careful planning, and I was eager to make a good impression. Mutti suggested a tongue roast would be a fitting meal for a special guest like Paul Raibourn. After all, he was the president of Paramount Television Productions and the moving force behind Paramount Pictures' early venture into television.

While tongue is not usually served on dinner tables in America, or listed on the menu of most restaurants, in Europe, it is a delicacy just as tasty and tender as any cut of beef. On the appointed day, Mutti ordered a three-pound calf's tongue from her butcher, and I spent the afternoon as her *sous chef*, preparing the evening meal.

When Klaus and Paul arrived, the table in our tiny dining area was set to perfection – damask linen, Havilland china, silver candlesticks, and crystal wine glasses. The guest seemed impressed, and the dinner progressed like a dream. First, an a*peritif* with the appetizer, then the main dish served in slices with gravy, asparagus, and scalloped potatoes.

After taking a few bites of the meat, Raibourn smacked his lips. “You’re a lucky guy, Klaus,” he exclaimed. “Your wife is a marvelous cook.”

“I can’t take the credit. Klaus’s mother helped me,” I admitted coyly.

“This meat is amazingly tender and delicious. What is this?”

“Calf’s tongue,” I answered. “Would you care for another helping?”

There was a short pause, as Raibourn fumbled with his napkin. “I think I’ve had my fill. It was delicious, thank you.”

The next day when I asked Klaus if Paul Raibourn had commented on the evening, he said, “I suspect Paul never ate tongue before, but you passed with flying colors.”

“And, by the way,” he chuckled, “Raibourn said we should move to a larger place. He’d see that I got a raise.”

***

CHAPTER 7

Opening Night

The year 1947 dawned as a time of great optimism about the future. Our nation's boys were home from the war; they were getting married, settling down, and starting families.

In Los Angeles, now home to almost 1.5 million people, land developers were snapping up farmland in places like the San Fernando Valley to start new subdivisions as the baby boom began.

It was the year Princess Elizabeth, heir to the English throne married Phillip Mountbatten; it was when the Dead Sea Scrolls were discovered and when Dior's New Look dominated the fashion scene, with its rounded shoulders, cinched waist, and very full skirt. It was also when Jackie Robinson became the first black player to break the major-league-baseball color barrier.

Our little "boomer" Clevie was almost a year old and a constant delight to Klaus and me. Klaus frequently traveled to New York as he prepared his experimental station to become KTLA, the first American commercial TV outlet west of the Mississippi. On those trips, he never failed to send his son postcards that expressed his love for this beautiful country. One pictured the Statue of Liberty.

"This is the Lady that gives newcomers a chance to live their dreams," he wrote.

One day Klaus surprised me when he announced, "I think we'll get you a car." I saw a dilapidated Model T Ford in a used-car lot and fell in love with it. Klaus's main concern was safety, so after upgrading it mechanically, we had it painted navy blue and the upholstery done in a tartan plaid, and Klaus had a high seat built for Cleve.

My son and I washed the little car almost every day and except for stalling often on Hollywood Boulevard, we had a great time driving around—just the two of us.

The Launch

In a later 1950 column, *Tele-Views,* a Los Angeles precursor to *TV Guide,* recalled that for the first time in Los Angeles history, a television station had opened its doors in 1947 to the commerce of the world. It read:

"It was a brave gesture, for there were no more than a paltry 1,000 television sets in the entire area and no more than a pitifully small handful of businessmen willing to invest hard dollars in what could only be called "a noble experiment at best." (*Tele-Views* may have been too generous with its count as others put the number of TV sets at 350.)

I remember KTLA's Opening Night with mixed emotions—both joy and anxiety.

As he left that morning, Klaus asked me to pick up his "good" suit at the cleaners and bring it to the studio later in the day, with with a fresh shirt. I kissed him good-bye and crossed my fingers, knowing the responsibility was weighing heavily on his shoulders. He mentioned he wasn't as worried about possible technical glitches as he was about how the "amateurs" who would perform. By that, he meant the celebrity participants who agreed to make an appearance but didn't know beans about working in front of live television cameras. And that included Cecil B. DeMille who delivered the opening remarks.

There were six cameras to be exact, all tweaked by the technicians to relay a clear, undistorted picture to the Mount Wilson transmitter eighteen miles away and viewable all the way from Santa Barbara to San Diego.

In piecing together the sequence of events that evening, I thank my parents, who lived in Brazil, for saving all my letters in those early years, and later delivering them to me to keep as a record of that stage in my life.

On January 16, 1947, I wrote:

> *Next Wednesday, the 22nd, will be an eventful day for KTLA (the new call letters of Klaus's television station). He has received the official permit to operate commercially, and it will mark its first sponsored program. Cecil B. DeMille, the famous film director, will give the opening speech. Bob Hope will emcee the variety show and a score of Paramount stars such as*

Dorothy Lamour will perform.

As you already know, the station has been moved outside the Paramount lot (next to the main gate), and soon they will build additionally to what is already a huge place. There will be a big cocktail party after the show and since I am the boss's wife, I will have to elbow my way among the celebrities and strike up the conversation here and there, which I dare say will be most interesting.

I shall keep you posted on the happenings of that evening."

While there were still relatively few TV viewers in Los Angeles, the studio was crammed with Paramount executives and bigwigs from major ad agencies whom Klaus and his bosses wanted to impress.

From the start, it didn't go well. Dorothy Lamour fell ill and dropped out at the last minute. Bob Hope was in a snit. Hope came to Klaus, waving his arms "What do I do? What do I do?

"Just look into the little green eye," Klaus told him, "and it'll go fine."

Hope, a veteran of vaudeville, movies, and radio—a man who had hosted the Oscars repeatedly since 1939— seemed so unprepared for this evening. At the appointed hour, announcer Keith Hetherington said, “This is KTLA, formerly W6XYZ television, Los Angeles, broadcasting on Channel 5. Good evening, everyone.” Then he introduced Bob Hope, who acted as if he’d been asked to play a game but didn’t know the rules.

Because Hope was accustomed to performing on radio, he appeared with a huge sheaf of papers in his hand—his script. He hadn’t memorized his lines, and there were no teleprompters or cue cards in those days. Hope barely made eye contact with the cameras as he shuffled his papers and stumbled through his emcee chores. In later years, he would become one of the first TV performers to use cue cards.

Bob Hope emcees KTLA’s Opening Night

“I wanna tell you, it’s a great thrill to be here on this wonderful initial program of station K-T-L,” Hope began, leaving the “A” out of KTLA, “And, ladies and gentlemen, this is Bob—first commercial tele- vision broadcast—Hope, telling you gals who tuned in, and I wanna make this emphatic, if my face isn’t handsome and debonair, please blame it on the static.”

That brought only scattered laughter from the audience. It was not Hope's finest hour, and he soon began to realize it. At one point in the proceedings, his eyes darted from camera to camera as he said, "All I wanna know is which one picks up the smell?"

Klaus and his staff had prepared an elaborate tropical background for the Dorothy Lamour number, but not everyone got the word that comic actor Eddie Bracken was subbing for her. So Bracken came on, doing a pantomime bit about a baseball pitcher but the setting looked like Waikiki Beach, not a ballpark.

Several performers failed to follow the script and missed their cues, leaving awkward "stage waits" in the show where nothing was happening in front of the cameras.

Because the Musicians Union was in the middle of heated contract negotiations with the broadcast networks, it had banned any live music performances on television. So singers on the KTLA inaugural broadcast had to use pre-recorded music in the background. Unfortunately, the performers and the music weren't always in sync.

Five days later, I wrote another letter to my parents, describing KTLA's debut.

> *It meant a lot of work, and I didn't see Klaus for two days, during which time he didn't sleep a wink. On the day of the show, I had to bring everything he needed to wear that evening. He did look smart.*

"From the audience's reaction it was a great success, but Klaus was a little upset because the reviews were not so good and, of course, he takes the responsibility for everything. The big stars never like to come to rehearsals, consequently didn't follow the script that was written for the show, and for which the cameramen were prepared.

The trade papers panned the KTLA opening night in the most vicious terms. *Variety* wrote: "Television went commercial on Paramount's KTLA last night, but as a show, it didn't go very far.

The medium, however infant, must suffer from comparison with its sisters, and on that basis, it was generally poor when not downright dead in an entertainment sense."

Columnist Jack Hellman went after Klaus personally: "You can't make a producer out of an engineer any more than you can make an engineer out of a producer," he wrote, calling the show "a crude, unpolished, thrown-together collection of acts."

Hellman said that Klaus had been "unprepared" to stage the broadcast, adding that the studio and the ad agency that represented the sponsor "should have engaged a director with stage, picture or radio experience."

I sent my parents my own review of their comments:

As I said before, from the viewer's perspective it was swell but from the reviewers' angle (a critical cut-throat bunch of newspapermen) it wasn't so professional as it should have been. Klaus, of course, took all the blame, and it was very unfair. I felt so sorry for him.

He was quite unhappy about it but believes every slap is a boost, and he is more determined than ever to surprise them.

So many people haven't yet enough faith in television. I guess those are the things we, the pioneers, have to endure. I was so proud of my husband."

Now for the light side. There was a wonderful cocktail party afterward, lots of chatting with the stars and surprising as it may seem, there were comments about your daughter that rather startled me. From a very important producer: "You are like a picture out of Vogue.*"*

Mama, I wore my black silk taffeta dress with a big bow at the back, white kid gloves, a matching pin and earrings (a birthday gift from Klaus)and two white gardenias in my hair, attached to a little black veil.

It would be sixteen months before W6XAO, the other experimental station in Los Angeles would be granted a commercial license, although it had been broadcasting for 16 years by 1947. Klaus had begun a tradition of beating the competition. He would also prove the critics wrong, demonstrating that he was a first-rate showman who would build KTLA into the dominant West Coast television station in those early years.

***

CHAPTER 8

A Deadly Brew

At first, it felt like an earthquake—a strong shaking beneath my feet accompanied by a low rumble. It was the morning of February 20, 1947. I was in the house and immediately rushed outside to check on Cleve, who was playing in the sandbox with a little blonde girl from across the courtyard. I was relieved to see they were still playing happily, blissfully unaware that anything out of the ordinary had happened.

Explosion at electroplating plant

When I called Klaus at the station to ask him if he knew what caused the rumble, he said there had been an explosion downtown, with casualties. He couldn't talk long, and said he was making plans to cover it live. Ground zero was the O'Connor Electroplating Corporation, located in the industrial area of Pico Boulevard just under two miles south of City Hall.

About 9:45 a.m., the company's chief chemist, Robert Magee, had been working on a technique he had devised for polishing aluminum. The family-owned business had hired the thirty-five-year-old Magee based on the extensive scientific credentials he presented, including degrees in chemistry and metallurgy. His bosses hoped that Magee's aluminum process would bring healthy profits to the company as it tried to grab a piece of the postwar economic boom in America.

Magee and his twenty-two-year-old assistant, Alice Iba, had mixed two highly dangerous chemicals, perchloric acid, and acetic anhydride, and poured them into a large vat. When they lowered a plastic rack into the liquid, things went horribly wrong. The plastic reacted with the chemicals, which produced a gigantic explosion that blasted a crater twenty-two feet wide by six feet deep. Seventeen people died that day, and 151 were injured. Magee and Iba were probably blown to bits; their bodies were never recovered.

The *Los Angeles Times* said the plant "exploded in an atomic-like eruption of smoke and flame." People felt it all the way from the Los Angeles Harbor to the San Fernando Valley as the blast devastated a four-block area, destroying or damaging 116 buildings, breaking windows in surrounding neighborhoods.

One news account of the blast described a fifteen-foot piece of twisted pipe being thrown over a four-story building, landing a block away, killing a ten-year-old boy riding his bike. Closer to the scene, a young man struggled to free himself as firefighters pulled the body of his father from the rubble. “Other workers were bleeding and moaning; some were tinted green by the chemicals,” the Times reported.

The shock waves reverberated with a deep roar some six miles away in Hollywood and rattled the studios of KTLA. As he barked orders, mustering his crew, telling the men to get the live transmission trucks ready to roll, Klaus made a decision. That evening’s programming, commercials included, would be pre-empted, and the station would sign on as soon as it could with continuous coverage from the scene of the explosion. Klaus expected nothing less than an “all-hands-on-deck” effort.

There was one major technical hitch. Klaus and his crew had designed the trucks to provide live picture transmission via microwave but hadn’t set up a similar link for the audio. Usually, when the trucks went to a remote broadcast, the station relied on the telephone company, AT&T, to transmit the sound via its network of copper wires. It had worked well for pre-scheduled events like baseball games and parades, where the audio lines could be ordered in advance, but not so well for breaking news.

"There was an hour delay in getting on the air," said John Silva, a former Navy radar officer hired by Klaus the previous year to run the station's remote broadcasts. In a 2007 account, Silva wrote about that day and said that all things considered, the phone-company people did their best. "This was quite fast," he said, " and they weren't set up for emergency service at that time."

Klaus was fuming over the delay, Silva said, mercifully leaving out whatever colorful language Klaus may have used. Silva said he immediately started working on a way to transmit audio as well as video without having to wait for Ma Bell.

KTLA had just started commercial broadcasts less than a month earlier and hadn't yet assembled a news department. Without a regular newscaster to anchor the coverage, Klaus tapped Keith Hetherington, the KTLA announcer, and the multitalented Dick Lane, both of whom had regularly performed on experimental broadcasts, to provide live commentary at the scene of the explosion.

Dick ad-libbed for hours at the site, interviewing eyewitnesses and describing the activity as fire crews and police looked for signs of any survivors among the rubble. With the coverage stretching into dinnertime, KTLA found itself "scooping" the morning papers as officials dropped by to provide a detailed account of the disaster. The immediacy of live television news coverage was something that print just couldn't match.

There were only a few hundred television sets in Los Angeles at the time, and the audience for the coverage was small, but KTLA attracted plenty of attention that day with those live pictures from the scene. Since the police were turning away thousands of gawkers at the blast site, the only way for the public to see what was going on there was via television. Anyone with a receiver was tuned to the station and gathering family and friends to come over to watch.

In March, a coroner's inquest would discover that Robert Magee, who had touched off the blast, was a fraud. He had no scientific degrees and in fact, hadn't even finished high school. A real chemist, the inquest concluded, would have known that the particular substances involved should never have been handled so carelessly. The incident led to stricter city and state regulations for dealing with dangerous chemicals.

Coincidentally, at the same time the inquest jury was releasing its findings, the Los Angeles Electrical Club sponsored "Television Week" to promote sales of TV receivers. It was a huge hit and every available set in Los Angeles was sold, with a backlog of orders for more receivers. By September, there were an estimated three-thousand sets in use with more being added every day.

Dick Lane went on to announce wrestling and roller derby for KTLA and pound fenders in countless car commercials. At the peak of his sportscasting career, Lane received about a thousand fan letters weekly. People loved his rapid-fire delivery and his signature exclamation, "Whoa, Nellie!" when the action got intense.

"It's show business," he said, "And that's the business I've been in since I was a little kid."

What KTLA did the day of the O'Connor Electroplating explosion transcended show business. A precedent had been set. That day would mark the first live television coverage of a major disaster anywhere.

I don't remember how late it was that night when Klaus got home, but I could tell he was very proud of how his guys had performed under immense pressure. From then on, whenever big news broke, he would move heaven and earth to get KTLA's live cameras to the scene, a tradition that continued long after he died.

***

CHAPTER 9

Who's on First?

By September of 1947, The Federal Communications Commission was mulling over a rule requiring television stations to program at least four hours a night. Klaus Landsberg was already doing that in Los Angeles, inventing all sorts of shows to fill the schedule.

Commercial TV was off and running, and Klaus was first out of the gate in Los Angeles. He knew he would have the competition breathing down his neck very soon as six other commercial stations were getting ready to sign on between May of 1948 and September of 1949.

As an independent station with no affiliation, KTLA would soon be up against outlets owned by the big networks, ABC, CBS and NBC—with huge bankrolls—but Klaus had an advantage over them. Because there wasn't yet a "live" coast-to-coast video hookup, and since there was no videotape in those days, the network stations relied on film recordings of live shows from New York. Employing something called the "kinescope" process, technicians used movie cameras to capture the images displayed on special TV picture tubes. That resulted in fuzzy, washed-out copies that the network stations would run a week after the shows had aired in New York.

KTLA was broadcasting the vast majority of its shows live, and Klaus was doing everything possible to make sure the picture was as sharp and clear as the technology of the day permitted. As viewers flipped channels, the difference between KTLA's live images and the week-old network kinescopes was dramatic.

Sporting events occupied much of KTLA's airtime, including amateur boxing from South Gate Arena, minor-league baseball with the Hollywood Stars, and wrestling from the Olympic Auditorium.

There were special events, like the championship rodeo from the Los Angeles Coliseum, an event staged by Gene Autry, then one of the country's most popular singing movie cowboys. It foreshadowed a long relationship between Autry and KTLA.

Another regular programing staple was disk jockey Al Jarvis, appearing three times a week, playing the hits of the day nine years before Dick Clark would host "American Bandstand" out of Philadelphia, and thirty-four years before MTV would come along. Jarvis used "soundies," three-minute musical films showing bands and singers performing popular tunes—the music videos of their day.

Long before shopping networks established a presence on cable TV, Klaus had a *Shopping at Home* show with Keith Hetherington and Harisse Brin, sponsored by some of the leading department stores in Los Angeles.

Sponsors who wanted to buy a half-hour of airtime on KTLA in 1947 were quoted a rate of $416. That included studio facilities and three hours of rehearsal. By comparison, the Dumont station in New York, WABD, was charging $705.

The early audience ratings were clear: KTLA was leaving the network-owned stations in the dust. The Hooper service consistently gave KTLA nine of the top 10 local shows. Tele-Q, another rating service, gave KTLA 19 of the top 25.

Klaus had proven the critics wrong, as a brilliant engineer and natural showman who would build KTLA into the dominant West Coast television station in those early years, and recruit a spectacular roster of talent to accomplish that task.

When *"Tele-Views"* magazine polled twenty-nine thousand Los Angeles readers in 1949, KTLA's shows were voted their favorites in nineteen out of twenty-five categories.

The top favorite variety show was *Western Varieties*, with Spade Cooley, beating the likes of Ed Sullivan and Arthur Godfrey, both on CBS. *Harry Owens and his Royal Hawaiians* took the top spot in the favorite musical show category.

"Hoppy" Rides Again

A KTLA cowboy show also rose to the top. When the readers of *Tele-Views* were asked to name their favorite western show, the answer, hands down, was *Hopalong Cassidy*. A year earlier, actor William Boyd, who had played Cassidy in a series of sixty-six movies, sold his ranch in Malibu to buy back his old films and the rights to the character for $350,000. He was betting the farm on the idea that a whole new generation of fans would discover "Hoppy" on television. Boyd first contacted KTLA since it was the leading station in the Los Angeles market and a place where he thought he'd draw the biggest audience.

While Klaus was building his schedule around live shows, he quickly recognized that the old Hopalong Cassidy films would play well on TV. They had a one-hour running time, tailored for double feature showings at movie theaters, but also perfect for a television slot. Boyd and "Hoppy" had a built-in audience of people who grew up with him in the '30's and '40's, and now *their* kids would also watch. The deal paid off handsomely, for KTLA, and for Boyd, who later signed up on other stations.

William Boyd as Hopalong Cassidy

In an article written by actress Joan Crawford in *Tele-Views* magazine, she revealed that while screening one of her old movies at home for her children, she noticed that her son Christopher had quietly left the room and was watching Hopalong Cassidy on TV in another part of the house. "The incident taught me something I've suspected for a long time," Crawford wrote, "that if I ever hope to be popular as an actress with my children, I'll just have to appear on a TV program."

The Debut of "Emmy."

One of Klaus's friends in the industry, writer, consultant and critic Syd Cassyd, had formed the Academy of Television Arts and Sciences in 1946. When he first came out of the service in 1945, Klaus hired him as a grip at KTLA, and the idea of a TV Academy was something they had spent many long hours discussing.

"When I first started thinking about forming an academy," Cassyd told me, "my vision was to create a democratic forum for exchange of ideas and dissent and to get all echelons of the still-infant industry, as well as educators, involved with the medium at its inception, grow with it and so understand it." The Academy wasn't yet a national organization, and its awards were limited to shows produced and aired in Los Angeles.

A discussion ensued over what to call the ATAS trophy. Cassyd thought the award should be called "Ike," after the iconoscope tube in the early TV cameras. But that nickname was already famously identified with General Dwight D. Eisenhower, so Lubcke suggested "Immy," for the image orthicon tube that replaced the iconoscope. Meanwhile, film editor Louis McManus, using his wife Dorothy as the model, had created a statuette depicting what the Academy called "the winged muse of art uplifting the electron of science." She was a beauty and needed a feminine-sounding name, so "Immy" was changed to "Emmy."

I had a head table seat at the first Emmys

The inaugural ATAS Emmy awards ceremony was staged on January 25, 1949, at the Los Angeles Athletic Club in Hollywood. Klaus and I were seated at the head table with Los Angeles Mayor Fletcher Bowron, who officially named that date as "TV Day."

KTLA won three of the six awards given at the event. A twenty-year-old ventriloquist Shirley Dinsdale with her puppet sidekick Judy Splinters received the very first Emmy ever handed out to anyone in television. Voted "Best Performer," Dinsdale had previously been on the radio with stars like Nelson Eddy, Rudy Vallee, and Eddie Cantor.

Mike Stokey, host of *Pantomime Quiz* (which featured celebrities playing charades) won an Emmy for "Most Popular Program," and station KTLA was also singled out for "Outstanding Overall Achievement." Three other awards were given: "Best Film Made for Television" to a half-hour adaptation of Maupassant's *The*

Necklace; an award to Charles Mesak of Don Lee Television for his invention of the phase fader, a device that could flip negative images into positives, and one to Louis McManus, for his appealing design of the Emmy symbol.

A few things stand out in my memory about that evening—the navy blue lace dress with a pink lining that Klaus purchased for me to wear, the klieg lights and flashing bulbs that greeted us on arrival after parking our cars, and the fact that the banquet tickets only cost five dollars.

That first Emmy ceremony, with six hundred guests and only a few celebrities, had little of the glitz and glamor that the awards have taken on in recent times. In 1997, I was surprised to be invited as a VIP guest to ATAS's glittery fiftieth Anniversary celebration and given the celebrity treatment. I was assigned a glamorous designer gown to wear that evening and a bodyguard to protect the fabulous diamonds, on loan from a Rodeo Drive jeweler, which encircled my neck. The Emmys had come a long way.

Back in 1947, Klaus knew that the networks were not going to stand still and let him run away with most of the accolades and a majority of the Los Angeles viewers. In fact, they soon stole two of KTLA's Emmy-winning performers, Dinsdale and Stokey, by offering them more money and the promise of national exposure.

A Pivotal Year

The competition was heating up in 1951—the year in which AT&T would complete its nationwide coaxial cable and microwave network that would carry television signals as well as telephone traffic from coast to coast.

No longer would Los Angeles be cut off from the East; those week-old shows could be aired the same night as they were broadcast in New York. The networks could also carry big events like the World Series live in every corner of the land.

On the news front, the Korean War was dragging on, and public opinion was deeply divided about the conduct of General Douglas MacArthur, who had been relieved of command in Korea by President Truman. MacArthur had let it be known that he disagreed with his Commander-in-Chief over whether to use air power against China, which was then fighting with North Korea against the American-led UN allies. Truman fired MacArthur because he thought the General was guilty of insubordination and was about to escalate the conflict into something that could lead to another world war. MacArthur's fans maintained that letting the general crush communism was worth the risks.

MacArthur's homecoming to San Francisco was going to be a big deal with thousands and thousands of people planning to greet him. TV broadcasters all wanted to cover it live, and it was then that Klaus got a taste of how intense the competition with the networks would become.

The San Francisco to Los Angeles leg of AT&T's microwave relay system was already up and running. When Klaus inquired whether the phone company could make the relay available on a pooled basis to all broadcasters who wanted to carry the MacArthur homecoming, he was told no. NBC had already tied up exclusive use of the one and only signal path from San Francisco to L.A.

When Klaus appealed to NBC to share facilities, the network scoffed at him.

"All right," Klaus said, "If that's how you want to play it, I'll build my relay."

He began talking to other broadcasters about borrowing some of their gear, which he planned to use, along with KTLA's microwave equipment, to send pictures of MacArthur's arrival to Los Angeles. He huddled with his engineers, plotting out the best mountaintops to use to beam the signal along a 350-mile path. Klaus told the other six LA stations that all of them would be welcome to use the link free of charge "as a public service." NBC, realizing that it would no longer be able to scoop the competition, relented and agreed to share the AT&T relay.

MacArthur arrived on April 17, 1951, to a tumultuous welcome with newspapers estimating that a million people lined the route of his motorcade from the airport to his hotel. The TV pictures were dramatic, but the General spoke very few words. He would save his valedictory—"Old soldiers never die; they just fade away"—for an address to Congress a few days later.

On September 4 of that same year, AT&T had its 3,000-mile hookup system working nationwide as President Truman journeyed to San Francisco to address the Japanese Peace Treaty Conference. This would mark the formal conclusion of U.S. occupation of Japan six years after Japanese forces surrendered to end World War II.

An estimated thirty million people watched this first live television coast-to-coast broadcast in the United States, with East Coast audiences impressed with the clarity of a picture sent from almost three thousand miles away. Thanks to Klaus's challenge to NBC a few months earlier, it was carried on a pooled basis, available to all broadcasters. The television industry has used similar pooling arrangements ever since on major news events when there is only one path to send a signal.

When praised for so doggedly getting his way, Klaus used to say: "I owe it to my viewers. They've been loyal to me for a very long time. I won't let them down."

***

CHAPTER 10

Everyone's Child

It was mid-October of 1987 when a message from TV editor Aleene MacMinn flashed across my computer screen at the *LA Times*.

"How about doing a piece for Calendar on the Kathy Fiscus telecast, with some recollections of your ex?" she wrote. "We want to run it with the rescue of Baby Jessica McClure."

In an event reminiscent of the Kathy Fiscus ordeal 38 years earlier, 18 month-old Jessica had fallen down a 22-foot well while playing in her aunt's backyard in Midland, Texas. She remained

Kathy Fiscus rescue scene in San Marino, 1949

trapped there for 58 hours. And once again, America's eyes were riveted on the television screen as the rescue unfolded on CNN, then a fledgling cable news outlet.

"The Fiscus tragedy happened ages ago!" I protested. "I would have to give it some thought. When do you need it?"

"You have three hours to deadline. Can you do it?"

"I'll try."

After digging into our newspaper archives, I began.

> *"They called it television's "baptism of fire" -- the event that would prove its power to communicate and hold its audience in the grip of the first major news coverage in the medium's history. It focused on tiny Kathy Fiscus of San Marino, a blond 3-year-old who, on a footrace with playmates, fell into an 110-foot abandoned well shaft only 14 inches in diameter. That unforgettable day was Friday, April 8, 1949...."*

That historic twenty-seven and one-half-hour telecast of the Fiscus rescue attempt on KTLA, Channel 5, had a profound and lasting impact on those of us who watched the drama unfold. I still remember the almost unbearable agony it engendered as we prayed that little Kathy, wedged in her rusty cylindrical prison, ten stories below ground, would be freed.

When I wrote my "flashback" story, the events surrounding the Fiscus telecast had become somewhat hazy in my mind, but after I had turned in the copy, Editor Barbara Saltzman surprised me with a message: "The piece is just terrific." To me, it seemed less than satisfactory.

Time and space did not permit me to expand on the story, as I can now, with recollections I have since gathered from scattered interviews with KTLA crewmembers who shared their personal experiences with me, among them Robin Clark, Stan Chambers, John Polich, Eddie Resnick, and Bill Welsh.

A Call for Help

Here now are my clearer memories of that Friday evening in April 1949. We had a hurried dinner, with constant phone interruptions as Klaus learned of the accident that happened late that afternoon.

Kathy had been playing with her older sister Barbara, nine, and five-year-old cousin, Gus Lyon, when she fell into an abandoned water-well shaft. Gus ran to the house to tell Kathy's mother what had happened. The police were called and within minutes, the first rescue units arrived.

The rescuers said that, at first, they could hear Kathy's faint cries from the depths of the well. Fire crews tried dropping ropes in hopes that the little girl could grab on and be hoisted out, but she didn't respond. They lowered air hoses to supply her with oxygen.

Volunteer crews from the 20th Century Fox Studio showed up with movie klieg lights to illuminate the scene at night. We went to bed that evening hoping and praying that Kathy would be freed by morning, but it was not to be.

After leaving for work on Saturday morning, Klaus called me from his office. “It looks like we're heading out to San Marino to cover the rescue of the little girl,” he said. "It may be more serious than we think. Pray that it'll be over soon. Don't know when I'll be home."

Kathy Fiscus

John Polich, who was in charge of remote programs, remembered having arrived at the station in Hollywood around 1:00 p.m. “We were getting our equipment ready to cover live wrestling at the Olympic Auditorium when Klaus came out of his office and told us to stand by,” he said.John remembered Klaus saying, a little girl is trapped in a well in San Marino.

A half hour later Klaus said, “They

still don't have her. I think we'll swing by the rescue site. If all goes well, we can still do wrestling." But John continued, "We never did."

Klaus assigned his sportscaster and special-events announcer Bill Welsh and a very young Stan Chambers, who was tracked down at the Biltmore Hotel, where he was emceeing a B'nai B'rith luncheon.

As the KTLA trucks pulled up at the scene, the rescue crews had dug two shafts parallel to the well casing where Kathy was trapped. They estimated Kathy was about ninety feet below ground and were using a rotary well-digging machine to extend one of the rescue shafts to that depth. The work, involving more than one hundred volunteers was intense.

Technical Difficulties

Klaus wanted to start broadcasting as soon as possible. But Polich realized there were a couple of hurdles to overcome. Because the trucks had no generators, he would have to beg, borrow or steal some power to get on the air.

Polich, a valuable crewmember—a man of action who would try anything that might solve a problem—said he spotted a lineman on one of the nearby electrical poles and yelled up to him.

"How about hooking up my power?"

"What d'you want, 220?" the man asked.

“Yeah, thanks!” John yelled back. And within minutes, the trucks were powered up.

But there was an additional electronic snag, Polich recalled. “There was no way to transmit video and audio on one signal, but Klaus was so shrewd. He figured it out, with an assist from John Silva and some duct-tape ingenuity."

Klaus had a pair of microwave transmitters, one of which he tuned in to a higher frequency for the picture signal and the other to a lower frequency for the audio. Never mind that the FCC hadn’t licensed KTLA’s equipment on those frequencies.

“In those days, you could infringe on somebody else’s signal,” Polich said.

So, in short order, the trucks were transmitting, with Eddie Resnick, Robin Clark and Jim Cassin behind the cameras.

As the broadcast was starting, Stan Chambers recalled Klaus speaking through the headset system he and Welsh and the camera operators were wearing.

“They are trying to cut open a window in the side of the well pipe to see if they can spot the little girl,” Klaus told them. “After that, they’re going to stop digging. I’ll have these monitors in front of me to see what is going on and I’ll tell you over the earphones what the camera is showing and you just describe it.”

For the rescuers, it was dangerous, grueling work. Water kept seeping into the rescue shafts and had to be pumped out. Drill bits kept breaking as the blades hit large underground boulders. The cameras recorded the comings and goings of the men as they were lowered into the ground and later hauled back up, completely exhausted.

And so it went for the next twenty-seven and one half hours: KTLA's reporters and crew members working in relays with Klaus in the truck calling the shots.

Kathy's parents, David and Alice Fiscus, stood frantically by. They had been only 250 yards away in their San Marino home when their little girl stumbled into the well. As the hours stretched on, the rescuers considered all sorts of possible schemes. The files of Hollywood Central Casting were being searched for little people who could be lowered into the pipe to reach Kathy. A thin man from the Clyde Beatty Circus and a tiny actor who played the bellboy "Johnny" in Phillip Morris cigarette ads volunteered, but neither was small enough to enter the fourteen-inch shaft. A jockey from the nearby Santa Anita racetrack was also deemed too big for the job.

Neighbors Gather

Again, in 1949 there were relatively few television sets in Los Angeles. Those of us who had them shared them with neighbors and welcomed total strangers who drifted into our homes to join in the Kathy Fiscus vigil.

Cecil Smith, former *Times* TV columnist, then a reporter covering the event, remembered driving home at dawn on Palm Sunday after spending time at the well site. Along the way, he observed a crowd of people at the window of a music store on Wilshire Boulevard. A TV set inside the window was tuned to Channel 5, KTLA.

"They were glued to that little black box, watching history unfold," he recalled. "It was the first time I had been aware of the impact and potential of the new medium."

In his memoir, Stan Chambers remarked that this one event sold more television sets than anything else, as it set the standard for live news coverage.

Fast forward to 1987: In Midland, Texas, the Jessica McClure drama ended on a jubilant note as rescue workers hauled the 18-month-old out of the well, bruised and scraped, but alive, her little head wrapped in gauze bandages. ABC, CBS, and NBC interrupted regular programming to join CNN in televising the successful rescue, in the perfect conclusion to a real-life TV drama.

But back in 1949, the Kathy Fiscus rescue attempt had no such happy ending. After rescuers had dug through to the place where Kathy was trapped, they discovered her lifeless body. Dr. Paul Hanson, the Fiscus family physician, went before the cameras and microphones at 8:53 p.m. "Kathy is dead," he said, "and apparently has been dead since she was last heard speaking on Friday." The crowd sighed and moaned as he spoke.

The Messenger

Bill Welsh later remembered being approached by Los Angeles County Sheriff Eugene Biscailuz when the live broadcast signed off. "He said to me, 'You know the Fiscus family was watching this on television until it got so sad they turned it off, and they don't know what's happened.'

'They know you, Bill,' he continued, 'so would you be willing now to go up to their home and tell them that the little girl is dead?' I said to Gene, who was my friend … 'Of course, I'll do it."

"So after the twenty-seven and a half hours of television, I went and called the Fiscus family together and told them that Kathy was just not coming home."

Across Los Angeles, groups of people who had clustered in front of television sets joined in mourning the loss. It created the greatest letdown the city had experienced together, with viewers brought close to the scene, watching every moment of the rescue effort unfold until its tragic final chapter. That day, tears flowed freely from the eyes of brave men who had risked their lives in the rescue effort, and throughout the city the people of Los Angeles were bonded in their grief.

During the long ordeal, Klaus, who never left the site, had me send a fresh change of clothing to him. When he finally returned home two days later, emotionally and physically drained, his face covered with a stubble of beard, I remember him saying, "This is so tragic, but it is also television history."

In an editorial dated April 12, 1949, *Daily Variety* editor Arthur Unger singled out the Kathy Fiscus coverage by TV station KTLA as the greatest job for the development and progress of television. "Klaus Landsberg and his boys," he wrote, "will never realize the important feat they accomplished for the advancement of television by the spot news reporting and visualization they did."

The well was sealed with concrete and capped off. The land later became an athletic field for San Marino High School. Observing the 50th anniversary of the tragedy in 1999, local civic leaders marked the location of the well with a bronze memorial plaque titled "For Kathy." It reads:

"Fifty years ago today, the miracle of radio and television transported our entire nation to this field. Here we witnessed the courageous attempts of so many to save the life of a little girl named Kathy Fiscus."

She was *everyone's* little girl.

***

Klaus with members of his “dream team”

CHAPTER 11

The Dream Team

By the early 50s, Klaus had succeeded in putting together one of the finest, most closely-knit television teams in the country. The station also built a deep feeling of affection and loyalty between itself and its audience by concentrating on locally produced live shows, while the competition was running canned programming from the East Coast.

KTLA's performers committed many on-air fluffs, but the audience always forgave them. The team carried it off by simply being themselves at all times on or offstage, They were dedicated to the medium and consistently ran off with enough top poll ratings and special awards to last a lifetime.

The dream team was anything but average. These newcomers quickly demonstrated their considerable talents in every area of programming: news, comedy, drama, sports, music, education, variety, and special events.

I wish I could profile each of these team members. They all deserve recognition as pioneers, such as the versatile announcer Keith Hetherington, and Jack Latham, a veteran news anchorman on NBC-TV in the 60s and 70s, who delivered the news on W6XYZ in the 40s.

Gil Martyn, among the best newscasters in the business, did his job as if his life depended on it. A KTLA anchor in the late 1940s, he would interrupt his fifteen-minute newscast each night to deliver a soup commercial, actually picking up a spoon and taking a sip of the stuff. I recently came across a note he scribbled to Klaus, with the heading: Thoughts during a Busy Day. "How proud and happy am I to have such an understanding and wonderful captain of my ship."

The Taskmaster

Not everyone felt the same about Klaus as Martyn did. Some called him *The Dictator*, others resented his frequent use of the phrase "you meathead," when out of frustration Klaus would point out some crew member's failing.

Newsweek magazine wrote about Klaus's quick temper in 1953: "Some of his detractors say that he terrorizes the people who work for him. One man who has worked for him for five years says: 'He never asks if something can be done. If you can't do it, he still wants it done.'"

In a recent phone interview, Bob Reagan shared memorable moments, when just out of high school he was hired as an usher at the KTLA Studio Theater, eventually becoming in charge of Guest Relations. "Everyone called Klaus by his first name, but he also demanded loyalty and obedience. When one of the ushers refused to climb a ladder to change the words on the theater marquee, Klaus summoned one of his directors, Gordon Wright, and the two changed the marquee. He fired the usher on the spot.

"Klaus was always very good to me. I was not part of his operating 'team', so I was never called 'meathead' or chewed out. Those who were not in fear of him loved and respected him."

Klaus's search for talent led him to the discovery of Lawrence Welk, who had been in the music world for some time but had never been involved with television. *The Lawrence Welk Show*, televised every Friday night from the Aragon Ballroom at the Pier in Santa Monica, became one of the most successful and fondly remembered programs in TV history. It featured musical numbers and skits, with host Welk leading the band, kicking off each tune with a thick German-accented "A-vun and a-two and a-three," and featuring Roberta Linn, his Champagne Lady, and accordionist Myron Floren.

While Welk was grateful to Klaus for giving him his first big break on TV, the two German immigrants were famously stubborn and clashed over the number of commercials in the show. After a year, Klaus decreed that commercial breaks would come in ten-minute intervals, instead of every fifteen minutes.

"Lawrence was very unhappy about the whole thing, to put it mildly," said John Silva, whom Klaus had tapped to direct the show. "He told Klaus that in no way was he about to change the show format."

But Klaus simply ordered the crew to cut into the show at the ten-minute mark for commercials. Lawrence didn't budge and kept on playing, although the band was off the air. The commercials ended, and the station cut back to Lawrence with egg on his face. The band had stopped playing, and the cameras awkwardly panned around the ballroom, showing the audience waiting for Lawrence & company to resume performing. After about a minute of this awkwardness, Lawrence introduced the next tune, and the show went on. The bandleader knew the battle was lost and for the rest of his time at KTLA, observed the Klaus Landsberg ten-minute rule.

KTLA stars Lawrence Welk and Spade Cooley

Big band remotes were among KTLA's most popular early offerings. Orchestra leader Leighton Noble, who played the posh hotel circuit from the Waldorf in New York to the Ambassador's Cocoanut Grove in Los Angeles, was the host of his show on station KTLA for six years. The program provided pianist Liberace with his first *Bandstand Revue* television broadcast appearance.

Though not with the high-powered versatility of a Milton Berle, Spade Cooley had only to take a fiddle under his chin and he automatically became the King of Western swing. The son of Dust Bowl refugees from Oklahoma and part Native American, he could trace his ancestry back to Geronimo. Sadly, Cooley's career ended in

1961 when he was arrested for the murder of his second wife and later sentenced to life in prison.

The charming and versatile image of Dick ("Whoh, Nellie!") Lane is indelible: a man with rare gifts and impressive credits who, as I've shown, was with Klaus from the very beginning.

Stan Chambers joined KTLA in 1947. This beloved and gifted newsman became a Los Angeles TV legend while serving as a reporter at KTLA for more than six decades. The USC graduate and Navy veteran first started working behind the scenes, but within a few months, he became a regular performer. Years later he would flatter me by remembering I was the one who nudged Klaus to put him in front of the cameras. Stan was too good-looking to remain in the backroom, I told Klaus.

Stan Chambers covers a refinery fire

Stan made a big impression when sent to cover the 1949 Kathy Fiscus tragedy, along with Bill Welsh, a veteran radio announcer, who made his television debut on KTLA in 1946 announcing hockey games. Welsh moved on to KTTV Channel 11 and later served as president of the Hollywood Chamber of Commerce.

The irrepressible Bud Stefan, another refugee from radio, was writer- director-producer of his show *Yer Ole Buddy* on KTLA. He described early television as a madhouse that required flying by the seat of your pants to pull it off.

"Saturday nights were the craziest. Tim McCoy followed Herb Wagner's dog show *Man's Best Friend*, and then I came in with my kids' show.

The crew sometimes didn't have enough time to change the sets and the live camera would have to focus on McCoy's co-host, American Indian Iron Eyes Cody, playing the tom-tom until the set was ready for me to perform."

Dick Garton also had a solid radio background and took over many of the announcing chores including the Tournament of Roses in Pasadena. Harry Owens was another show business veteran I remember well. He was an expert on Hawaiian music who had never taken the trouble to study it and write it down.

Owens came up with the Harry Owens Royal Hawaiian Show, first heard at the Waldorf Astoria in New York, then at the Saint Francis Hotel in San Francisco. The show, a regular feature on KTLA starred the lovable hula dancer and comedienne Hilo Hattie.

Korla Pandit, a handsome young musician with a mysterious ancestry, became an overnight sensation on KTLA in 1949, playing romantic compositions, both on the organ and a grand piano simultaneously. Klaus spotted Korla at a furrier's fashion show in a Hollywood restaurant and offered him his own daily television show, *Adventures in Music.*

Korla Pandit, the mystic entertainer

Their contract agreement stipulated that Korla would not speak a word during the show and would always wear his jeweled turban. Also, he would provide musical accompaniment for *Dixie Showboat*, *Frosty Frolics*, and Bob Clampett's popular show *Time for Beany*, featuring Stan Freberg and Daws Butler as puppeteers and voices.

For the next five years, Freberg, Butler and Pandit performed live, five days a week, 52 weeks a year, including Christmas and New Year's Day. The show's principal characters were Beany, a plucky young boy who wore a beanie; the brave but dimwitted Cecil the Seasick Sea Serpent, and the pigheaded Captain Horatio Huffenpuff.

Time for Beany became the number one children's show, while also appealing to adults, including Albert Einstein, a huge fan. He reportedly once ended an important meeting with scientists at the

California Institute of Technology by saying, "Pardon me for leaving, gentlemen, but it's Time for Beany!"

Beany and friends aboard the *Leakin' Lena*

Children also watched Rose Marie Iannone, a child actress whose show Sandy Dreams, debuted in 1948. Other kids' favorites included Tom Hatten, an afternoon host, and artist who doodled and ran Popeye cartoon shorts from the Paramount library, as well as Frank Herman, "Skipper Frank," a ventriloquist whose show was also filled with old movie cartoons.

Another popular KTLA crewmember was Sherman Loudermilk, a former Marine Corps combat artist who impressed Klaus with his work and was hired as art director for Channel 5. He was a whiz at creating real-life settings and built, and painted sets for such shows as *Dixie Showboat* and the ice-skating variety show *Frosty Frolics*. When Klaus decided to do a Western show for children, Sherman found himself unexpectedly assuming the persona of "Cowboy Slim."

Klaus wanted a "real" cowboy, and Loudermilk fit the bill; he was a strapping six-foot-two Texan who had been raised with horses.

When asked who was going to be the host, Klaus said, "Loudermilk, of course. He's from Texas."

Mystery fans watched John Milton Kennedy and H. Allen Smith in *Armchair Detective*, a show that ran in 1949 and 1950.

Dorothy Gardiner, a former Conover model who had been breaking into television, paired off with Keith Hetherington and Ken Graue on *Handy Hints* and later on *City at Night*, and was a popular KTLA performer for several years.

Behind The Scenes

The engineers were among the hardest-working members of the dream team—all infinitely well qualified, who brought with them diverse experiences from serving in the military. Those I remember the most are Ray (Pappy) Moore, Jim Duncan, Vincent Filizola, Roy White, John Silva, Bob Physioc, Hec Heighton and Charles Theodore.

The cameramen were also a diverse bunch of great guys. Eddie Resnick, an experienced meteorologist, joined W6XYZ in its earliest days, as did my friend to this day, Robin Clark. Others included Jim Cassin, Walter Vukoye, Bill Barnard, Gary Westfall, and Dick Watson.

Who could ever forget the intrepid John Polich, former captain of the Monarchs hockey team and All-American in football and hockey. He could be trusted to tackle the most demanding and daring assignments, and he became one of Klaus's closest friends. My son Cleve remembers John as a proxy father after Klaus passed away, and to this day remains close to his daughters and their families.

In other responsible jobs, Klaus relied on the creativity of his program directors Gordon Wright and Phillip Booth, a British aristocrat who immigrated to California. There were scores of others who contributed so much to the success of the station.

Few women held regular jobs at W6XYZ and KTLA in earlier days, but in addition to the regular female performers such as Ina Ray Hutton and her All-Girl Band, the Champagne Lady Roberta Linn, puppeteer Shirley Dinsdale and Dorothy Gardiner, there was Ethel Doris Frederick, the first and only female engineer and production equipment operator. Others I remember as deserving of recognition as pioneers in the field of television include Ethel Greenfield, Jeannie Karaganus, and Klaus's longtime secretary Irene Carroll.

When Cleve and his wife Catherine gathered many of the members of the Dream Team together in a 1985 reunion, many left tape-recorded memories of their early days. Karaganus may have summed it up best: "It was a thrill and a joy and a delight, and sometimes a pain in the neck to work with Klaus, but we all loved him very much."

***

CHAPTER 12

The Breakup

There had never been a divorce in our family and I was struggling with a guilt-ridden conscience, unable to disclose even to my brother, my strongest ally, that I was unhappy: that I was a wife without a husband, and even beginning to doubt my self-worth.

Rare visits from relatives or friends from Brazil were always joyous occasions. They were anxious to meet this brilliant guy, rumored a genius, whom I'd married. I would take them to the station to meet Klaus, who was always gracious but rarely sat through dinners I planned for our guests.

By the time I was ready to serve dessert, the chair at the head of the table was empty, Klaus had excused himself and was back at work, although he left our guests fascinated with television.

"Does your husband ever take a vacation?" was a recurring question.

TV reporters often referred to Klaus's unusual lifestyle. In a *Tele-Views* issue on January 20, 1950, columnist Dan Jenkins wrote: "Klaus Landsberg works a minimum of 14 hours a day, and the word 'work' is used advisedly. He hasn't had a vacation in twelve years. His weekends are at best half-day affairs, and he seldom gets home before midnight, if not later."

One night Klaus arrived home and was met by two police officers at our front door. They told him a man had tried to break in through our bedroom window. "Your wife was here alone with your kid. A neighbor alerted us. Where were you?" asked one officer, indicating I could have been raped. Klaus was so upset that the next day he hired a carpenter to reinforce the locks and windows throughout the house.

Our little three-year-old filled my days. We had great fun together. I taught him how to ride his tricycle, took him to the park, told him stories and delighted in simply watching him grow, but the nights were long and lonely, and the only adults in my life were Klaus's parents and an elderly couple who lived in a small bungalow on the property. To us, they were Aunt Pearl and Uncle John, two wonderful people who insisted on taking care of Cleve so I could take classes at the nearby Barnsdall Park Art Center.

At that time, I was more limited on outings. I no longer had my little Model T Ford that I had gotten from Klaus. He said it was no longer safe to drive, and we sold it. Soon we'd get me a new car, he promised, but our budget was still pretty slim.

I was eager to explore my creativity and took up silversmithing, sculpture, gem faceting and leather tooling. I also discovered the Reginald Denny hobby shop close by on Hollywood Boulevard that specialized in model airplanes and ships. I've always enjoyed putting things together, and assembling those little models became my favorite pastime after I put Cleve to bed, and while waiting for Klaus to return home, usually around 2:00 a.m.

One evening as I was struggling with the rigging on a mini replica of Sir Francis Drake's *Golden Hind*, I stopped and asked myself, "why am I doing this?" I suddenly felt strangely disconnected, and immensely sad. The next day I called Dr. Herman Abraham, the Landsbergs' German physician, who still made house calls.

When he arrived, he asked me how I felt.

"I don't know," I said. "I just feel very sad."

He checked me over and then said, "I'll give Klaus a call and have him come home right away."

"Oh, don't … he's so busy."

"That's the problem," said the doctor as he dialed the phone. "He's much too busy."

In less than ten minutes, Klaus was home, looking anxious as he rushed to my side.

"What's wrong, Baby?"

"I'm OK … I'm not dying."

"She is not OK," interrupted the doctor, wagging his finger at Klaus. I still remember his words. "I want you to listen carefully, Klaus. Your wife is like a beautiful flower that is wilting for lack of attention."

"Evie knows how much I love her," he protested. "She also knows I'm building a future for us."

"She misses you, Klaus. You must make more time for your family."

Klaus promised to rearrange his schedule, and for several months, he kept his word.

His parents offered to watch Cleve more often so I could accompany Klaus to work-related functions. I was alive and once again feeling like a helpmate to my husband. Letters to my parents reflected the joy and happiness I felt. I even convinced Klaus to take a trip to Brazil, so I could introduce him and Cleve to my extensive family and my beautiful native country.

I did visit my family in Brazil, but without Cleve or Klaus. He simply couldn't take time off and resisted my taking Cleve, reminding me of a pact we had made early in our marriage, based on the alarming frequency of plane crashes.

We agreed that the two of us would not fly together unless we took our child, for fear of leaving him an orphan, should there be an accident. If only one of us flew and something happened, at least one of us would be left with our son.

I suspect Klaus also feared I might want to remain with Cleve in Brazil. That would never have happened, but he may have sensed my eagerness to be involved in creative projects outside of my marriage.

During my stay in Brazil, I obtained a job as a Hollywood Foreign Press correspondent for *O Cruzeiro*, a major Brazilian entertainment magazine. Klaus was pleased for me, but that still didn't fill the void created by an absent husband.

Meanwhile, Klaus was adding new programs to KTLA's schedule. *Fun on the Beach* was staged on the weekends, and each week Dorothy Gardiner, a show participant, stopped by to pick up Klaus, who always took Cleve along to play with John Polich's kids. The wives stayed home.

I was not the jealous type, but neither was I thrilled to see a pretty girl in a convertible drive off with my husband and son for a fun day at the beach.

I felt left out. I could appreciate that Klaus was intent on building a future for his family. But, what about living the present?

My brother Richard, then living in Los Angeles, was the first to notice my decline in weight and spirit. He urged me to consider the pros and cons of my unusual lifestyle. He also understood my desperate need to spread my wings.

The straw that broke the camel's back was a phone call one morning from Irene Carroll, Klaus's secretary.

"There is something you ought to know," she began, hesitantly.

"Has something happened to Klaus?"

"No… he's fine. But there's a rumor spreading."

"What rumor?"

"That Klaus is cheating on you."

"That's impossible. He'd never do that." At first, I was angry that Irene should even mention such a thing. Her words were hurtful, but I also knew her as a good friend. She meant well.

"How did it this rumor get started?" I asked.

"You know how Klaus is—always the last one to leave the station. He likes to check on all the equipment. And every evening

Dorothy waits around until he's finished, and they leave together."

I was still making excuses for him. "After leaving the station, he always goes to Oblath's to eat." In those days, Oblath's was the unofficial commissary for the Paramount crowd.

"That may be true, but people are talking. I'm so sorry."

I had heard of women cozying up to their bosses for special favors, but when I confronted Klaus, he brushed it off as vicious gossip.

"You know I don't like eating alone," he said. "Dorothy is good company and all we do is talk business." But I felt I should be the one to fill that need for companionshp.

We'd met Dorothy in 1948 at Earl Carroll's Nightclub, an early Hollywood landmark, famous for its slogan: *"Through these portals pass the most beautiful girls in the world."* Klaus was hoping to strike a deal with entrepreneur Carroll on a new, short-lived show titled *The Sky's the Limit,* featuring his star performer Beryl Wallace. Dorothy would also be involved with the show.

It was shocking to all of us when we heard that Earl and Beryl were killed in a plane crash en route to New York, on the night the show was aired. Ironically, a charred script of *The Sky's the Limit* was found at the crash scene. It was at this point that Klaus hired Dorothy.

My decision to leave Klaus did not hinge on a rumor but on my survival. The warning signs of an impending breakup were like an early morning fog that would momentarily shroud the sky, and then just as quickly clear up as the sun took over. I never blamed anyone for the breakup. It had more to do with whom I needed to be.

Loyalty, the strongest of my values, was being put to the test. Finally, one morning I walked away with our four-year-old son, leaving my wedding ring and a note on the dining room table.
The note read,

I've given a lot of thought to our marriage, and how beautiful it could have been. My decision to end it now is neither careless nor hasty. I feel I no longer have a husband, and cannot be the best mother to our son unless I find my self again. Cleve and I are staying at a friend's home in Alhambra, and I will call you from there. I still love you and will always be your friend.

My choosing to end our marriage was inconceivable to Klaus. He felt betrayed and pleaded with me to come to my senses. "Forget this foolishness and return home so we can be a family again," he'd say. My parents also pressured me to reconsider. But, I simply needed to move on.

Earl Murphy, my lawyer and my brother's best friend, had arranged for me to stay with his mother who owned a bungalow court in the quiet suburb of Alhambra.

Each night after my little boy fell asleep; I would untie the blue ribbon that held Klaus's love letters and cry myself to sleep reading them.

I felt a deep sense of loss and tortured myself by dwelling on the verses of that old nursery rhyme: "Humpty Dumpty sat on a wall;

Humpty-Dumpty had a great fall. And all the King's horses and all the King's men couldn't put Humpty-Dumpty back together again. My heart was broken, and I felt it could never be put back together again. The magic was gone.

Mrs. Murphy became my tower of strength during that difficult transition. She was an admirable, no-nonsense woman. I remember sitting with her at her kitchen table listening to her uplifting words. "One can always find, a way to be gra-a-a-nd," she'd say, stretching the word in her thick Irish brogue. "Preserve that natural optimism, girl, and you'll be fine. You'll be grand. Just wait and see."

I wrote my parents.

There have been wonderful moments in our marriage and the decision to break it is the hardest decision I've had to make – but I also believe it will turn me into a stronger woman.

I still have the fragile paper on which my father wrote his soothing reply.

Occasionally we had a feeling that perhaps the home life you were leading was not quite so perfect as your brave words implied. Too great a workload could not ensure that bonding so necessary in a home of two brilliant young lives.

The seeds were good and the soil first-class, but the necessary, careful tending with physical presence and communication of ideas and sentiments, has evidently been lacking. However, "there is a turn in the affairs of man" (Shakespeare), which is ordained by a Superior Being or Power, and so long as one has not committed any grievous fault, things generally work out for the best. Meanwhile, you can count on our warm solidarity and love --100%. Put on a stiff upper lip, and have confidence in yourself.

I think my father understood that while I wanted to live in that house with a picket fence, I may not have been ideally suited for it unless it was also connected to a vast field of possibilities I needed to explore within my community.

Moving On

Bulky Speed Graphic cameras and popping flashbulbs hemmed me in on my day in court. Though I was not a celebrity, there always seemed to be some news value in anything gone amiss in the showbiz circles of Hollywood. When asked, "Why are you divorcing?" I could only reply, "I was a wife without a husband."

The next day, one newspaper headline read "Latin Beauty Sheds TV Exec." It seemed such a callous way to end a cherished chapter of my life.

After my divorce, I remained marginally close to the KTLA scene. Klaus kept me posted on the station's progress when he came to my apartment in Alhambra to pick up our son for weekend visits.

Cleve was the center of our lives and Klaus and I were always cordial with each another.

Cleve, the center of our world

It was not until a few months later that he called me one morning sounding like a lost child. I was startled. I thought something had happened to Mutti or Vati, my in-laws.

"I've just been to the doctor," Klaus said. "They've diagnosed me with malignant melanoma. Do you know what that means?"

"I don't."

"It's the fastest-spreading form of cancer." He sounded desperate. In the early 1950s, the word "cancer" was still considered unmentionable. A cancer diagnosis was like a death sentence. Klaus did not want to believe he might die. He was only thirty-six, a young man with so much he hoped to accomplish.

"Let me help," I told Klaus. "Let me at least get you a list of the best specialists. There's always some breakthrough in medical research." I called the Sloan-Kettering Cancer Institute in New York and spoke to an oncologist who confirmed that malignant melanoma was the most dangerous form of skin cancer. But, what was the prognosis?

Melanoma had a poor survival rate in the 1950's, and the statistics were not encouraging. Life expectancy was a maximum of five years, depending on how soon the symptoms were detected. It was now a question of whether the melanoma had progressed beyond the original site and reached the lymph nodes. In the course of dealing with such questions, there were moments when I regretted leaving Klaus. I felt he needed me.

"I should have listened to you and Mutti," Klaus moaned.

Looking back on earlier days, I would say that the best time to chat with Klaus was early in the morning, while shaving in the bathroom, stripped down to his shorts.

Perhaps it wasn't the most romantic setting, but those were blissful moments when he seemed totally detached from his work, and pleasantly involved with trivial matters and telling me jokes he'd just heard.

I'd stand behind him watching him in the mirror, as he stirred the foamy cream in his shaving mug and then lathered up his cheeks with the fluffy white blobs.

"And a ho-ho to you," he'd laugh when I called him Santa Klaus. He would tell me how much he treasured the little cobalt blue shaving mug I made for him in my ceramics class, and I was surprised years later that it still occupied a place on his bathroom counter.

The mug had a man's face in relief, lathered up in cream. On its bottom I had inscribed our private code—a nostalgic reminder of Klaus's earlier days with NBC, the network's audio signature: "Bing, Bang, Bong." It was our way of saying, "I love you," when in a crowded room.

Aside from becoming an expert in the art of shaving, it was during those bathroom meetings that I first noticed the dark spot at the beltline on Klaus's back. Both his mother and I kept urging him to have it checked, but he never seemed to find the time.

Klaus would undergo seven cancer operations in the next five years, and except for close friends, very few people were aware that he had any serious health problem. Television was the blessing that kept him going and rewarded him in ways that nothing else could.

***

KTLA's cameras at first televised atomic bomb test in Nevada

CHAPTER 13

They Said It Couldn't Be Done

Klaus had just recovered from his third cancer surgery in early 1952 when he was handed a task that would have daunted most healthy men. Could he pull off something that others had deemed impossible? It all went back to events that had taken place the previous year.

While Klaus was busy helping to usher in the Television Age, the world was also in the frightening beginnings of the Atomic Age. The US monopoly on atomic weapons had ended when the Soviet Union tested its own A-bomb, raising fears about a potential Soviet nuclear strike on the American homeland. "Civil Defense" became a much-used buzzword in those days.

Our son Cleve remembers the "duck and cover" drills at his school, when children were told to seek shelter under their desks—a questionable protective measure in the event of an atomic blast.

The United States was building up its stockpile of nuclear weapons to counter the Soviet threat. And, as part of the buildup, the Atomic Energy Commission (AEC) began conducting regular tests of nuclear bombs, first at Eniwetok Atoll in the Marshall Islands of the Pacific, and later, closer to home.

On January 11, 1951, the AEC disclosed what up until then

had been top-secret information: the establishment of its new continental nuclear test site in an area in southern Nevada, sixty-five miles north of Las Vegas, buffered from public access by federally owned dry lakebeds, and larger than the state of Rhode Island. Headquarters for the whole operation was a military-style encampment known as Camp Mercury with armed sentries at all the gates.

A Distant Flash

After the first atomic tests in Nevada in January of 1951, Klaus scheduled a one-hour news special on Tuesday, February 6, based on expert predictions that the nuclear bomb set to explode on the desert that day would be so powerful that it would probably be visible in the skies throughout the West.

By positioning a camera atop the 5,800-foot Mt. Wilson, 275 miles from the Nevada test site, he could offer a live view of the distant explosion, however dim. He sent newsman Gil Martyn to Las Vegas to give an audio account, and Dick Lane to Mt. Wilson with cameras to describe the scene. With typical optimism, Klaus also interrupted a cooking program the day before to announce what he had in store for his viewers the next morning at 5:00 a.m.

An estimated thirty thousand Los Angeles residents, including myself, were up at dawn to witness in amazement the eerie parabolic glow that lit up our screens. The image, lasting only a few seconds, was all that the "line of sight" could deliver but, despite our recent divorce, just knowing that Klaus had succeeded was an emotional moment for me.

Klaus had something bigger and better in mind—putting his cameras closer to ground zero for some future bomb test. He grew more confident that he could do it after successfully televising the US Marines' homecoming from Korea on April 29, 1951. It was a difficult challenge that involved sending a microwave signal 100 miles from Point Loma overlooking San Diego Harbor to KTLA's Mt. Wilson transmitter. At that time, Klaus's microwave relay was the longest ever attempted, using equipment that was designed to send signals only about forty miles.

Encouraged by that electronic "first," Klaus sent a filmed copy of the telecast to AEC officials, saying that if the opportunity were afforded, KTLA would like to participate in the coverage of an A-bomb blast, live from the Nevada desert.

He had tossed the gauntlet.

The Challenge

Klaus was not the only one lobbying for a closer look at the A-bomb. As Charter Heslep, the AEC's man in charge of dealing with broadcast media, later put it, "Newsmen became insistent that they be let in on one of these detonations. They said it was unfair that some members of Congress and the Armed Services were allowed to see these 'shots'—as we call them—and then have *their* stories printed, broadcast, and televised."

By November of 1951, the tension between the AEC and the media had escalated. Washington finally agreed to let news organizations, television included, into the Nevada proving ground.

The only question was "when?"

On the afternoon of Friday, March 28, 1952, AEC's Heslep made a conference call to the networks and to Klaus, whose "firsts" in the industry were well known. The group was given the green light to cover an A-bomb test, but with some hurdles to clear.

The test would be on April 22, leaving only 25 days to prepare. The clock was ticking.

Running Interference

On April 1, at the Chicago convention of the National Association of Radio and Television Broadcasters, Klaus and other TV executives met with Heslep, who reiterated the problems that broadcasters would face, while adding a couple of new complications.

"For one thing, AEC uses dozens of frequencies in its operations, and none of the media may use a frequency that might interfere," he said. "This automatically bans the use of about 75 percent of the field equipment licensed to radio and TV by the Federal Communications Commission."

Heslep pointed out that interference from an electric razor once almost delayed a shot and added that, to avoid any mishap, it was crucial for a "rehearsal" to take place before the shot with all the TV gear in operation. The AEC set its frequency test for April 20. The TV people now had only nineteen days to get ready.

Las Vegas in 1952 had no television facilities whatsoever. That meant that a microwave relay was needed to link Yucca Flat, Nevada, to Mount Wilson in Los Angeles, the nearest pickup point for the AT&T transcontinental TV system. Spanning the 275 miles would require setting up relays over the snow-capped mountains and hot deserts of Nevada and California. Could the longest television remote pickup ever attempted be completed in time to provide the nation with the first live coverage of an atomic detonation?

Broadcasters were counting on AT&T to bridge the gap, but the phone company was pessimistic. By the end of the Chicago meeting, the networks chose Klaus to act as the group's technical director to deal further with AT&T.

On April 3, the phone company announced it was backing off. It would be impossible to complete the project within the required time. They estimated they'd need ten to twelve relays at a cost of $90,000 for its share of the work—a job that would require several months to complete.

Klaus's gut feeling was to try it on his own, but could he count on Paramount to agree to what seemed like such a gamble? He called his boss Paul Raibourn at Paramount in New York and detailed his plan. "I think I can do it on $40,000 and maybe get the networks to pitch in for half the cost," he told him.

Raibourn didn't hesitate. "We'll back you up, Klaus, even if we lose. Good luck!" Nor did the networks hesitate to accept his proposal or his leadership. They agreed to participate and share in the costs if the outcome was successful. Klaus assured them that if he failed they would not have to pay. It was now Friday, April 4.

That day, Heslep wrote his wife Margaret, in one of several letters that are now part of the Special Collections Archives of Oregon

State University, about the progress of the TV experiment:

> *"The telephone company has said that it will not attempt to produce a live TV signal. But this has not daunted the resourceful Klaus Landsberg. He already has found one mountain that can be used and is now working his way up toward our Mercury camp. I still fear the odds are against him, but cannot help admire his courage."*

Heslep would later state in a speech that "Those sixteen days would be filled with let-downs, strained backs and the courage of the engineers and cameramen of KTLA, who took on that challenge revved up by their leader, Klaus Landsberg".

A Long Shot

Klaus had already set up his first relay point for the hookup on Mount San Antonio, twenty-four miles east-northeast of Mount Wilson. Never mind that the snowpack was eight feet deep and that one had to use snowshoes to walk around. There was a cabin where the crew could hunker down, and Klaus and his men placed their transmitter and dish antennas nearby and established a signal back to Mount Wilson.

The next day, Klaus turned up at Camp Mercury. He told Heslep he was stumped for his next relay site and said they'd have to do some exploring.

Armed with an assortment of topographical and aerial maps, Klaus, his chief engineer Ray Moore, and remote-control engineer John Polich took Heslep on a bumpy ride across the desert in search of a peak along the jagged Clark Mountain Range. On April 7, Heslep wrote to Margaret:

> *We drove 286 miles on our 13-hour jaunt in a rattling Dodge power wagon to help Klaus Landsberg find a TV relay site on Mt. Clark some 55 miles southwest of Las Vegas. The search was unsuccessful, so I arranged for an aerial reconnaissance flight that had to be scrubbed due to 80-mile per hour winds.*
>
> *After that, Klaus, Ray Moore and John Polich were back on the desert driving around from mountain to mountain in Klaus's dusty black Chrysler.*

"We finally spotted a suitable shelf at about 6,200 feet on an unchartered peak and decided to keep the location a secret," Polich later disclosed. "We called it Mount X. The problem was getting the heavy, cumbersome equipment and supplies up that razor-backed peak. We could only do it by helicopter."

Klaus contacted the commanding officer at El Toro Marine Corps base and was told their copters had never been higher than five thousand feet. But like Heslep, the Marine general was caught up in the challenge and through the chain of command and Heslep's high-level connections got clearance from the Pentagon to dismantle two huge Sikorsky HRS-2 choppers, fly them from Chicago to the West Coast and reassemble them for use in the TV operation.

It was Wednesday, April 9, just eleven days before the deadline. By then, word of the television venture spread among the

Klaus and crew lugging a microwave dish to the Marine helicopter.

three thousand technicians, scientists, and military personnel at Camp Mercury, and bets were being taken on whether television would win or fail.

The risky attempt to lay out a 275-mile microwave relay across the California desert had become the second most popular topic of conversation in camp. At every meal in the crowded mess hall, Heslep was besieged with questions. “What’s the latest on the TV guys?” and “Can Landsberg pull it off?”

On Thursday, April 10, 1952, with ten days to go, the helicopters landed at Valley Wells, a small town close to Mount X.

Wearing parachutes, four KTLA crewmembers—Charles Theodore, John Polich, Faye Konkle and Klaus—were on the first flight to the mountaintop, and in the course of twenty-four additional flights, with four Marine pilots taking turns at the controls, they landed six tons of equipment, set up camp on the six-thousand-foot shelf, and kept their fingers crossed.

Polich recalled how fiercely his boss tackled the job: “I can still see Klaus, pushing himself terribly trying to meet the blast deadline set by the AEC. He had just undergone the third of seven operations to stem the cancer that wracked his body, and the strain of climbing caused the wound to bleed again.”

In spite of strong winds and freezing temperatures at night, the crew worked tirelessly around the clock and managed to get a signal across to Mt. San Antonio, 140 miles to the southwest.

It was now Friday, April 11. Klaus called Heslep with positive news, but the jubilation quickly turned to anxiety when the TV crew discovered that their signal was fading in and out.

In another letter to his wife, dated April 12, 1952, Heslep again expressed his concern for the TV project:

The television story has come to a most sad climax. Landsberg got his relay working on the 160-mile hop but it would not deliver a good picture after 7:30 AM, due to atmospheric conditions in the desert. He asked us to put the shot back to 7 AM.

I took up his request with the scientific staff, and we threshed it around quite a bit because everyone is rooting for this guy who will never say, "It cannot be done." Logistics and scientific requirements made it impossible to grant his request. Our decision had nothing to do with inconveniencing governors, VIPs, and reporters.

Not in recent years have I had to make a call more regretfully, and what do you suppose Klaus said? "Well, Charter, if that is the way it must be, I'll have to do some more figuring." He may make it yet. We all hope he does.

It would take them until Tuesday, April 15, to solve the problem and by then, there were only five days left until the dress rehearsal. The men returned to Valley Wells and left one brave crewman, Joe Featherstone, to watch over the equipment.

On April 16, Heslep wrote his wife:

Wonderful news. I was called to the radiotelephone from Charleston Mountain about an hour ago by Ray Moore, Klaus's chief engineer, to say they have a TV signal strong and clear from Angels Peak in the Charleston range, all the way to Los Angeles.

This is thrilling news, but last night at 11:35 PM, things looked bleak again. Landsberg, Moore and I were up on Angels Peak—9000 feet high and was it cold. Burr-r-r-r-r. We were in the radio shack that AEC had there. Klaus had put in a relay on Sloan Mountain about 18 miles from Las Vegas.
We could see everything in Las Vegas—even make out the hotels and gambling casinos—but no light from Sloan. It turned out that the maps were incorrect and a ridge not shown on the map blocked line of sight. The engineers thought they had that all important line of sight to Angels Peak".

So back to the drawing board for Klaus and his engineers. Heslep continued:

Everyone here stops me to ask how "the Dutchman" is making out. Will he succeed? An FCC man who was talking to our communications people said Klaus was regarded in professional radio TV engineering circles as a genius. I hope he gets the credit he deserves for the feat if it is successful.

The huge microwave dish antennas had to be re-positioned until Klaus found a small "slot" in the mountain ranges that permitted the signal to beam through without interference. It was now April 19, just one day before the dress rehearsal, and Klaus and his crew had succeeded. At 6:00 p.m., they had a clear signal all the way from the test site to Los Angeles!

KTLA truck at "News Nob" site, ten miles from ground zero

But then, foul weather moved in. A sandstorm swept through the test site, and it began snowing heavily at Mt. San Antonio. At the same time, a blizzard hit Mount Charleston and by 10:00 PM, the microwave relay was knocked out.

Finally, the blizzard subsided at Mount Charleston, and the crew got the big dishes lined up and operating again. The crew on

Mount San Antonio shoveled about a foot of snow and they, too, were back in business after a mostly sleepless night.

The next day, the dress rehearsal went perfectly. The AEC could find no interference from the television equipment. All communications on the agency's many frequencies were loud and clear.

KTLA had four cameras, equipped with special filters and 20 different lenses to cover the blast from a place the AEC had dubbed "News Nob," a rocky point just 10 miles from ground zero. Two hundred press representatives gathered there to witness the event, which they nicknamed "Operation Big Shot."

Moment of Truth

The decisive moment had arrived. KTLA started transmitting pictures at 8:45 a.m. on Tuesday, April 22, and the networks picked up the coverage by 9:05 a.m. And then, just when everything seemed to be humming along, the power failed at the test site at 9:16 a.m., knocking out all the TV cameras with just fourteen minutes left until the bomb was scheduled to go off. It spelled disaster for Klaus and his team—all their work for nothing! With Klaus yelling, "Somebody fix it!" several engineers scrambled around to get the power back on, but to no avail.

However, Klaus had a backup plan and a man who would save the day. He had established a fifth camera on Mount. Charleston, forty miles distant, manned by Robin Clark, who had the only picture at the moment of the blast.

At the appointed hour, 9:30 a.m. on April 22, thirty million Americans watched the historic first from the comfort of their living rooms—live pictures of an atom bomb blast, direct from Yucca Flat. After Robin had caught the initial flash, the cameras at News Nob were up and running a few seconds later. Robin said the moment he caught the bomb going off was the highlight of his professional life.

Newsmen Grant Holcomb, Gil Martyn, and Stan Chambers provided on-scene commentary for the TV pool.

"Beautiful, tremendous, an angry spectacle," Chambers described the scene as the cameras showed the ominous mushroom cloud rising and spreading above the Nevada desert. The viewers simply weren't aware of the fretful moments the TV crew had endured in the lead-up to the "big shot."

The Aftermath

Participants in the telecast returned to Las Vegas to a heroes' welcome. Bartenders on the Strip celebrated the detonation by serving up *Atomic* cocktails—a concoction of vodka, brandy, champagne laced with a dash of sherry—and the people danced to a then-popular boogie-woogie tune titled the "Atomic Bomb Bounce."

Bob Reagan, only 19 at the time, was assigned to entertain the press covering the telecast. "The waiters would have to bring the drink tabs to me outside the casinos because I was not old enough to be ordering at the bar. I'd sign the tabs and charge them to publicity head Howard Wormser (Room 475)."

John Polich later told me that when Howard handed Klaus the bill, he "raised holy hell". Klaus had obviously underestimated the ability of the press corps to run up a huge bar tab.

Tough Luck

It would be several months before the Marines could return with their helicopters to help KTLA's crew dismantle the equipment on Mount X. That effort, on November 21, 1952, turned into a near-disaster. The following day, Klaus recalled the misadventure during an interview:

> *Our equipment had been stranded atop the 6200-foot desert mountain peak we named Mount X, and Sikorsky HRS-2 helicopters were the only possible means of transporting equipment from this altitude.*
>
> *With cooler weather now prevailing in the desert, early this morning we sent a crew of KTLA technicians on two Marine Corps helicopters from Squadron 363 of the 36th Marine Helicopter Group from Santa Ana to Nevada to transport KTLA's equipment back to civilization.*
>
> *One of the helicopters, while attempting to land on the narrow ridge undershot its aim, presumably because of downdrafts, and in trying to lift itself back into the air, its tail rotor was caught and sheared off by desert brush or rocks. The helicopter lost control and rolled down the side of Mount X.*

By some miracle, the pilot, Major Dwayne Lengel, and co-pilot Capt. Gaylord Durtknecht, escaped with a broken tooth and minor bruises. KTLA team members John Polich and Faye Konkle were strapped to their seats in the cockpit and remained unhurt.

Walter Cronkite of CBS, a network member of the pooled coverage taking directions from Landsberg through his headset, later gave his version of the impossible feat and of the man who directed him throughout the telecast:

"Landsberg seemed to have an immediate grasp of the needs of the news business, as well as the vision of the possibilities of live TV coverage. He certainly was one of the geniuses of the early days of TV. He refused to accept anything as impossible."

And that is the way it always was.

***

CHAPTER 14

When the Earth Shook

Californians live with the reality that sooner or later the land beneath their feet will twist, rumble and roll as Mother Nature puts her underground house in order. We have even learned to joke about it.

But in the early hours of July 21, 1952, when all of California shook—from the Golden Gate to the Mexican border—it was no joking matter. That day, the small mountain town of Tehachapi, 120 miles northeast of Los Angeles, was awakened by the worst earthquake ever recorded in Southern California. What we experienced, to a greater or lesser degree was the largest earthquake in the United States since the one that destroyed San Francisco in 1906.

I awakened abruptly 4:52 a.m. when the quake rolled me off my bed onto a plush rug on the floor. I grabbed my robe, dashed to the backyard and stood alone, trembling, and terror-stricken. I had never been in an earthquake before, and as the earth rolled, I hugged the broad trunk of a huge magnolia tree and waited for what seemed like an eternity for the tremor to subside. It lasted for about a minute.

After the first shock, I made my way back into the house to get to the phone. My thoughts were focused on my son Cleve who was in Hollywood, spending the weekend with his Dad. At that time, I lived in Alhambra and worked for the local newspaper, the *Post-Advocate.*

Even before I could reach the phone, it rang. It was Klaus, wanting to know if I was okay and assuring me that all was well at his house. I was relieved and grateful for his call. Two hours later he called again, and it didn't surprise me when he said he was leaving for Tehachapi to cover the disaster. What did surprise me was that he wanted to take our son with him. Cleve was only six years old.

I argued that it was too dangerous to have a small child running around in the midst of all the pandemonium. "The crew and I will take good care of him," he assured me. "I promise we won't let anything happen to him. Don't worry, Evie. It will be a great experience. It will give him a real sense of how we work on remotes."

"What about the aftershocks?"

"He'll be all right. I'll put him on the phone. Clevie, tell Mummy bye-bye."

"Don't worry, Mummy," Cleve said with boyish excitement and sounding very much like a chip off the old block. "I'm a big boy now. I'm going to help my Daddy."

Klaus could be very persuasive and rarely took no for an answer. In spite of my concerns, I knew Cleve would be in good hands. The crew would be watching over him, as they usually did, whenever Klaus took him on remotes. I relented with some misgivings.

My preoccupation with safety for my son kept me glued to the news all day.

The *Los Angeles Times* reported that at its epicenter, just south of Bakersfield and only ten miles from Tehachapi, the quake measured 7.7 on the Richter scale, affecting 160 thousand square miles. The stricken railroad town, nestled in the mountain range separating Northern and Southern California, was immediately declared a major disaster area, and all emergency units, public and private, were mobilized, hampered in their rush assistance by landslides on the ridge route and other principal thoroughfares.

In those early days of television, there was always some new challenge ahead, but I never doubted that whatever Klaus set out to do, he would accomplish. I never ceased to admire his tremendous drive, energy and the improvisation that went into each of these demanding remote set-ups, especially since live coverage was still a pioneering effort.

I recently asked my adult son, "What do you remember of that earthquake, Cleve? You were only six years old. Were you scared?"

"All I can remember is that my Dad woke me up at dawn, slipped me into my jeans and a jacket and then placed me in the back seat of Bronco (the name Klaus gave his cars). I was still drowsy and must have slept the entire hour and a half it took to get to Tehachapi. My Dad was driving very fast, and we were in Tehachapi before the crew."

It seemed the only time Klaus could spend with his son was while working. "The KTLA studio was my playground, and its crew reluctantly assigned as my guardians. I got to go on many remotes—the Rose Parade, *City at Night*, you name it," said Cleve.

"I clearly remember being taken to Knott's Berry Farm for a show and waiting there for my Dad to arrive by ambulance from the hospital after an operation, and then taken back by ambulance after directing the show. Nothing ever seemed serious enough to keep him away."

"On the Tehachapi assignment, my Dad put Robin Clark in charge of me. He was a great cameraman, and I liked him. We're friends to this day."

Robin, who was first hired by Klaus when he was just out of high school and again after he returned from the Army, provided a vivid image of the 1952 quake.

"I arrived at work that morning and told to get ready to leave for Tehachapi. Klaus had already left, and we were to follow as quickly as possible. John Polich tied our aluminum antenna to the roof of my truck, and Jimmy Cassin, also a cameraman, and I loaded our truck with the equipment.

"All we used on remotes were the International Harvester bread trucks because they were roomy and enclosed. On one side we had the transmitter on a stand and on the other we had the sync-generator/power supply for each camera. Behind the seats were the console, monitor and control panel. The cameras, each weighing 100 lbs., stood at the back end.

"I was driving fast. The wind was strong, and the antenna suddenly blew off the truck. We turned back and drove about a mile to retrieve it. When we stopped for gas, there was the KTTV truck, so we hurried. Further along, we spotted the CBS truck, and then I hit the pedal and sped.

"When we arrived in Tehachapi Klaus was beaming. He gave me a bear hug. 'I'm so proud of you. We're the first on the scene.' Our engineers, Charles Theodore and John Silva, had already set up the equipment. Since there was a power outage, each remote had a generator and lights, so you had these pools of light traveling the roads."

"Klaus had taken Cleve along, and made me responsible for him," continued Robin. "The best way to keep Cleve out of mischief was to give him a job. He liked being part of the team. I gave him a headset, connected it to my audio and put him in charge of the mike line. I told him, I need you to let the line out slowly as we move along, and if we need to back up, I want you to gather it in slowly."

"Did he do a good job?" I asked Robin.

"Cleve was a bright little guy. He remained focused. He wanted his Dad to be proud of him."

"That night, everyone was so exhausted. We plopped on the ground in a park nearby, not knowing where else to sleep. Then, suddenly out of nowhere, a group of monks in gray habits showed up carrying soft quilts and blankets and laid them on the ground for us. I remember seeing Cleve fast asleep rolled up together with his Dad in those cozy quilts that the angels in gray had brought us. The next morning the monks had set up a long table and served us a delicious breakfast."

Survivors Remember

Recently, my co-author George Lewis went to Tehachapi in search of additional material for this chapter. He found that the Tehachapi Heritage League had a photo of one of the KTLA remote trucks on the scene of the devastation and that many of the old-timers still had vivid memories of the quake.

KTLA truck on the scene in Tehachapi

"I thought it was an atomic bomb," said Dick Johnson, whose father owned the local newspaper, the Tehachapi News. The paper's office was destroyed in the earthquake, but the Johnsons were unscathed. Father and son kept putting out the paper, using printing facilities in nearby towns.

"I didn't think it was going to stop," said Hugh Vasquez, who noted the shaking was so strong he couldn't get out of bed. "The church bells kept ringing," said Pat Gracey, who woke up to find her house tilting off its redwood pilings.

Longtime Tehachapi resident Del Troy remembered she happened to be in Long Beach on the day of the quake and that she was glued to KTLA's coverage, waiting for the mayor, Gus Koutroulis, to give a briefing on the extent of the damage and the toll of human casualties in her hometown. Since phone lines were down, news from Tehachapi was hard to come by, and KTLA became a vital information link that day. Most newspaper and radio reporters had no way of filing from Tehachapi and had to drive for hours to find working telephones.

The next day, the *Los Angeles Times* was filled with harrowing eyewitness stories.

"The earth rocked convulsively," said one man. "Entire faces of buildings on the main street crumbled and fell into the roadway. The lights went out. Men, women and children poured from the wrecked buildings. They screamed, moaned, and crouched in the streets."

Paul McGrath's iron lung quit due to the power cutoff, and he stopped breathing. He was saved just in time when the power returned.

The Quintana family wasn't so lucky. Pete Quintana, a welder and a miner, had arrived in Tehachapi the night before for a family reunion. People currently living in Tehachapi still remember how the

Quintanas hired a mariachi band to help celebrate and how happy they were that evening. Pete Quintana's wife and eight children were buried under the debris of the quake, and neither she nor four of the children survived.

Bodies of victims were not cleared from the wreckage for four and one-half hours. Most were buried under several feet of bricks, timber, and metal. On that day twelve persons were killed, eighteen were hospitalized, and several hundred were given first aid treatment. The 417 inmates and staff of the Tehachapi Prison for Women escaped injury and were evacuated. The building itself was declared unusable.

Wave effects from the tremor were widespread, with structural damage reported as far as Las Vegas and San Diego, according to a news report. "High tension power lines snapped like threads sending eerie blue flashes into the predawn sky, and severe oil fires blazed from Bakersfield to Long Beach. Water tanks in several communities cracked, and oil storage tanks near the Ridge route sprang leaks that sent a stream of petroleum flowing down the highway."

Some of the most violent shakings occurred along the route of the Southern Pacific Railroad about sixteen miles northwest of Tehachapi. The U.S. Geological Survey noted that tunnels with eighteen-inch thick concrete walls were cracked and that the quake "bent the rails into S-shaped curves."

Throughout the Los Angeles area, water splashed from swimming pools and damage to tall buildings, while superficial, was costly. Chickens were screeching in Arcadia; burglar alarms short-circuited, creating a terrific din in the business districts; church chimes rang in discord, and a church steeple careened into the street in Glendale. At Owens Lake, one hundred miles from the epicenter, the salt beds shifted. At the *Los Angeles Times* library in downtown Los Angeles, a six-ton storage-shelf section fell against another, causing a major cleanup job.

The California Institute of Technology at Pasadena recorded 188 aftershocks of magnitude 4.0 and higher through September 26, 1952; six aftershocks on July 21 were of magnitude 5.0 and higher, keeping people's nerves on edge for a long time. California residents were once again reminded to always have a first-aid kit handy and learn how to use it, to keep a three-day supply of food and a filled container of water in the refrigerator, and to learn how to draw water from the water heater if needed.

I've kept that in mind ever since.

***

CHAPTER 15

Bittersweet Sunday

Until a week before the Baby Miss America Pageant at the Hollywood Bowl, I had no idea our babysitter had entered my two-year-old daughter Terry in the competition. And as I look back, it is hard to imagine how that single day, September 6, 1956, could be so joyous, yet so sad.

Ironically, the event came as a blessing in disguise. It helped dispel some of the anxiety we all felt over the mounting seriousness of Klaus's illness. That week my 10-year-old son asked me, "Is my Daddy going to die?"

None of us wanted to believe that Klaus might soon be gone. We prayed for a miraculous turnaround that would help him beat the odds, as he had done before, following each of seven cancer operations. Most people were never aware of his illness. He wanted it that way.

It had now been five years since I had divorced Klaus and married Terry's dad, Don De Wolfe. Meanwhile, Klaus had built a home on El Contento Drive just over the hill from the Hollywood Bowl and shared it with his new bride, Janice McDonnell, also the parent of a young son John.

Janice was a member of a popular singing trio, the McDonnell Sisters, with sister Jackie and cousin Lou. They joined KTLA in 1953 and were popular performers on the *Ina Ray Hutton Show* and *Bandstand Revue*.

Three years earlier, after his third operation, Klaus asked me for more time with Cleve. By then I was a fulltime reporter at the *Los Angeles Times* and agreed to have our son attend school in Hollywood during the week and be with me on week-ends. in Alhambra.

The McDonnell Sisters. From left, Jackie, Lou and Janice

It was a workable arrangement. Klaus had a live-in housekeeper, Ida Batiste, whom we all trusted. Cleve also enjoyed being dropped off at KTLA after school and given a free run of the station; he was often mischievous but always condoned by a lenient Dad. "I don't know how the crew put up with me. I was a real brat," Cleve has said, chuckling.

The Sunday event at the Hollywood Bowl was enjoyable, more so since our little Terry emerged as Baby Miss America of 1956, winning over two hundred other contestants. Amidst an aura of triumph, we drove to Klaus's house, just over the hill from the Bowl. Cleve couldn't wait to show off his little sister. "I knew she would win," he told his Dad, and he took her by the hand to see him.

Klaus now occupied a makeshift bedroom on the ground floor of his home. He was only barely able to lift his head for a glimpse of the little champion in her yellow organdy dress and wearing a blue satin sash that proclaimed her the winner. He smiled and showered her with praise before lowering his head to the pillow.

It was a brief visit. Klaus was hooked up to a life-support system, looking pale and weak, but his eyes were bright and his mind alert. His courage was never so apparent. I held his hand gently after being cautioned that the slightest pressure might stop the flow of the intravenous infusion. He was still hoping for that last-minute reprieve. It was heartbreaking to see him so ill—a man continually on the go, who always felt so lucky.

I came across a letter he wrote his mother after she suffered a stroke en route to visit her son Peter's family in Israel. She remained in Amsterdam for several weeks in the care of friends, and Klaus wrote or called her every day. "You will soon recover and be good as new," he wrote, "I know that because I was born with a *glückshaube.*

I was intrigued. I looked up the German word *glückshaube.* It mea nt a "lucky hood", and referred to infants born within an amniotic veil, like a hoodie covering the head and face and sometimes the entire body–said to occur in one in 800, 000 births.

Supposedly, children born with a *glückshaube* are special, endowed with a heightened awareness and destined to serve humanity. Klaus was in famous company. Notables born with a *glückshaube* included Albert Einstein and Napoleon Bonaparte.

Unfortunately, Klaus's lucky streak would soon run out. He died at 40, married only seven months and with a new baby on the way.

I was grateful for the private moments Janice offered me at such a strenuous time. I wanted to reassure Klaus of my enduring friendship.

"How can I help?" I asked.

"Always tell Clevie how much I loved him," he began, "and please watch over Mutti and Vati. They love you like a daughter."

Klaus went on to say how painful it was to leave Janice alone and pregnant, and never to get to know his second child. "More than anything, I want to feel that my children will grow up as friends. You can make that happen, Evie."

That bittersweet Sunday was the last time I would see Klaus. By Tuesday, Mutti called suggesting I pick up our son. "There is little hope left for my Klauschen," she said. The following Sunday, on September 16, 156, the phone rang. This time, her message was brief and stoic. "It's over."

How does one tell a young boy that his Daddy is gone forever? There is no best way to deliver that kind of a pain to a child. You simply do the best you can.

I found Cleve in the bedroom fussing with his toys. “You know how very sick your Daddy has been,” I said. “He doesn’t deserve to suffer like that.”

“Huh, huh,” Cleve muttered, reluctant to hear what more I had to say.

“God didn't want your Daddy to suffer anymore, so he took him to heaven where he can watch over him. He won't be back.” I didn't know what more to say.

I watched my little boy fling himself on the bed, clench his fists and pound the pillow, his face buried in it as he tried to suppress his uncontrollable sobbing. He seemed angry to be left without his Daddy. None of it made any sense. I pulled him into my arms and tried to comfort him.

We talked about how we had both lost someone we loved dearly. He had lost his Daddy, and I had lost a best friend. “Now I’ll be your Mommy, your Daddy and your best friend; all rolled into one. How about it?”

Cleve managed a faint smile, and we hugged some more. Later we drove to the park, gloves and bat in hand, and played ball. I don’t think I ever felt any closer to my son than on that Sunday afternoon.

Three months later when Klaus Franz Landsberg was born, Janice told me that she and Klaus had chosen John Polich as the baby’s godfather and wanted me to be his godmother.

We were now one family.

Every local newspaper and trade publication in the West made mention of his death and praised Klaus’s accomplishments, his uniqueness, and courage. The day after his death, the Los Angeles City Council adjourned in memory of Klaus, identifying him as "one of the most important factors in making television history in the West."

Of the many tributes, I felt the most significant one came from his competitors – as a public announcement in the media issued jointly by Los Angeles stations KABC-TV, KCOP, KHJ-TV, KNXT, KRCA and KTTV.

> *The television broadcasting industry of Southern California and television as a whole have suffered an irreparable loss in the untimely passing of Klaus Landsberg.*
>
> *From the day, he came to Los Angeles when television receivers were few and the potential of the television camera virtually unknown; he devoted unceasing energy and skill to the progress of television. His contributions to the medium have been specific, important and lasting.*

***

CHAPTER 16

The Legacy

The *LA Times* called it "one of the most surreal moments in the history of Los Angeles criminal justice." And the fact that 95 million Americans got to watch it live on television is a testament to the legacy of Klaus Landsberg.

On Friday, June 17, 1994, the Los Angeles Police were planning to arrest football legend O.J. Simpson for the murders of his wife Nicole and her friend Ronald Goldman. They told his lawyer to have Simpson surrender by 11:00 a.m. But Simpson fled, accompanied by his longtime friend and former football teammate, Al Cowlings.

Then, that evening, Simpson the fugitive was spotted in his white Ford Bronco, driven by Cowlings. As the Bronco headed up the freeway toward Simpson's home in Brentwood followed by 20 or so police cars, a squadron of news helicopters joined the chase. Soon, the white Bronco appeared on television screens all over the country.

Domino's Pizza would later state that its deliveries that night would equal those of a Super Bowl Sunday as people found it impossible to tear themselves away from the coverage.

Eye In The Sky

The idea of using a helicopter as a TV-camera platform was something Klaus had envisioned many years earlier. In July of 1949, he decided to try it out when the station arranged for a remote broadcast from an aircraft carrier, the USS *Valley Forge*, a mile off the Southern California coast.

KTLA truck hoisted to flight deck of *USS Valley Forge*

Cameraman Robin Clark remembers driving KTLA's mobile truck from the station to the Santa Monica Pier, then heading south along the beach for a rendezvous with a Navy landing craft:

"They took me in the truck across choppy waters to the USS *Valley Forge* aircraft carrier, one mile out at sea, and hoisted us on to the flight deck. Klaus was already on board with his other cameramen, Eddie Resnick and Jim Cassin and engineer Charles Theodore."

With the help of the skipper, they decided to try placing a camera in a helicopter to get a bird's-eye view of the ship. "Klaus picked lightweight Eddie Resnick to go up with the camera on his lap and the dangling cable," Clark said. "The camera weighed 100 lbs., so we took off the viewfinder and got up to about 200 feet. Since Eddie had no viewfinder, Klaus gave him audio directions on where to focus."

I remember Klaus telling me how excited he was about the experiment. He referred to it as having "an eye in the sky." A few years later, he deployed the "eye in the sky" concept to get an aerial view of the Northrup Aviation plant in the suburb of Hawthorne. It was demonstrated during a *City at Night* show featuring the booming aerospace industry in Southern California.

Once again, lightweight Resnick was tapped to operate the camera. To further save weight, the camera's viewfinder -- the small TV monitor mounted on top of the camera body -- was again taken off to lighten the load.

John Polich, who served as floor director for the remote later remembered his instructions to Eddie: "We'll put the camera on your lap. We'll tell you to tip it up, tip it down, move it right, move it left."

Once again, the camera was tethered to the ground by a long cable that sent power to the camera and received a video signal in return. If the chopper flew too high, there was always the risk that the camera could be yanked off Eddie's lap and sent crashing to the ground.

The men on Klaus's team shared his vision and his love for experimentation that took the technology to the next level in 1958. Two years after Klaus's passing, one of those men, John Silva, got an inspiration while navigating through traffic on the Hollywood Freeway.

"If we could build a mobile news unit in a helicopter," Silva said in a 2002 interview for the Archive of American Television, "we could get over it all, get there first, avoid the traffic and get to all the stories before anybody in the competition."

This presented its own set of challenges. First, Silva, Roy White, and others on his team would have to cut that umbilical cord that tied the camera to the ground.

"All we had to do was condense two-thousand pounds of equipment down to four hundred pounds," said Silva, "and figure out how best to transmit a picture from an airborne mobile unit in a practical and economical manner."

Silva had become chief engineer of KTLA by 1958. His World War II training in radar technology made him the perfect man for the job.

Working with engineers at General Electric, Silva's team designed a microwave transmitting system that would be light enough to mount in a small helicopter, yet have a signal sufficiently powerful to send a picture from anywhere in the Los Angeles metropolitan area to the station's transmitter on Mount Wilson.

Directional dish antennas, normally used to concentrate microwaves into a beam, were no good, as the picture would fade whenever the helicopter changed course. Silva and his associates had to come up with a omni-directional antenna that would still have enough transmitting power to do the job.

Engineer John Silva with actor Gregory Peck in a publicity shot for the KTLA "telecopter"

Vibration was another big problem. In one of the early tests, Silva had to lean out of the helicopter to re-seat vacuum tubes that had been rattled loose in the trans-mitter. Afterwards, he and his team devised a system of shock absorbers and cushions to dampen the vibration.

Finally, on July 24, 1958, the "eye in the sky," now re-christened the "KTLA telecopter," was ready for its on-air debut. It was a great achievement. Audiences saw live pictures of the freeway system, the Los Angeles City Hall and the LA Coliseum, where the chopper landed and linked up with ground-based units.

It was a lovely summer evening in Los Angeles with no big breaking news to report. But there would be plenty later on:

On November 6, 1961, a huge wildfire erupted in the hills of Bel Air, one of the priciest neighborhoods in Los Angeles. While other stations struggled to get their remote units close to the place where the flames were consuming homes, the KTLA telecopter was overhead, beaming back dramatic live pictures. The coverage lasted 19 hours with pilot-reporter Larry Scheer and cameraman Harold Morby in the chopper and Clete Roberts, Bill Stout and Stan Chambers reporting from the ground.

The video was even more dramatic when, on December 14, 1963, the dam at the Baldwin Hills Reservoir, seven miles southwest of downtown Los Angeles, burst, releasing a quarter million gallons of water. The torrent killed five people and destroyed 277 homes. From the very first moment, as the wall of the dam was breached, the telecopter was overhead, and the coverage may have saved lives, alerting people to the impending disaster.

On August 11, 1965, rioting broke out in the Watts neighborhood of South Los Angeles. It started as a protest against the arrest of a black motorist by a white police officer and escalated into six days of chaos. The KTLA helicopter flew above the rioting, capturing the burning buildings, the police and national guard troops patrolling the streets and looters taking merchandise from stores. Some of the rioters didn't want to be on television and began firing at the telecopter, forcing it to operate at a higher altitude from the action.

For its comprehensive coverage of the riots, KTLA received one of the highest honors in television, the Peabody Award. The accompanying citation read, "A Peabody Award is presented to television station KTLA, Los Angeles, for its strategic news coverage during the critical period of the Watts riots when 30 persons were left dead and hundreds injured. Channel 5's Telecopter kept officials constantly informed; often served as the only check on new or isolated outbreaks; and, presented a graphic, moving close-up of the tragedy."

The TV news helicopter had proven its worth. By 1968, ten years after the telecopter's debut, other television stations were joining KTLA in the skies and by the year 2013, the number of news helicopters nationwide was estimated at between 100 and 120.

Sports Potpourri

Another part of the Landsberg legacy was sports. Klaus loved sports and loved showing sporting events on TV. In the early days, there was no major league baseball in Los Angeles, but minor league clubs like the Hollywood Stars filled up the airwaves.

When Klaus couldn't secure the rights for the bigger sporting events, he turned to what were called "fringe sports." KTLA in the late '40's and early '50's carried roller derby, where roller skaters would grapple with one another as they raced around an indoor track; destruction derby, where drivers crashed old cars until only one was left running; and something called "moto-polo" where drivers in dune buggies equipped with huge rolover cages would try to push a ball into a goal. It may have been "fringe," but the ratings were huge.

But the biggest Landsberg legacy in sports was the televising of professional wrestling.

The early wrestling shows on KTLA, recorded on film and syndicated to stations around the country, became a huge hit, coast to coast. Television turned the likes of Gorgeous George, Mr. Moto, Freddie Blassie, "Lord" James Blears and "Baron" Leone into major stars.

Never mind that the action was scripted, choreographed and quite hokey at times. The audiences loved it and still do. Today, World Wrestling Entertainment Inc. (WWE) says it reaches 36 million viewers in more than 150 countries. And it all started when Klaus put professional wrestling on the air back in the '40's. Equally popular was KTLA's annual telecast of the Rose Parade in Pasadena, which was first aired in 1947 and has continued uninterrupted every year since. To this day, KTLA's coverage attracts the lion's share of worldwide viewers.

After singing movie cowboy turned entrepreneur Gene Autry bought KTLA in 1963, the station got the rights to televise the ballgames of another Autry property, the Los Angeles Angels. The Angels would make KTLA their TV home for thirty-two seasons. The Los Angeles Lakers appeared on the station in the mid-70's, and the Dodgers joined the KTLA lineup from 1993 to 2001. Autry carried on another part of the Landsberg legacy, the country music show. Just as Klaus had presented Spade Cooley and Cliffie Stone's *Hometown Jamboree*, Autry starred in *Melody Ranch* from 1964 to the early 70's.

Passing The Baton

A living part of the Klaus Landsberg legacy are his two sons, Cleve and Klaus Franz Landsberg, andKlaus's granddaughter Amry Landsberg.

Klaus's star on Hollywood Walk of Fame

Cleve is a film producer and production manager. In 2010, he received the Frank Capra Award from the Directors Guild of America for his career achievement and service to the Guild.

Klaus Franz is a multiple Emmy award winner as one of television's most accomplished sound mixers. His daughter Amry is also following in the family footsteps and has begun a career in television production.

Today I can picture some tourist walking along the streets of Hollywood checking out the stars embedded in the sidewalks honoring the greatest names in film, radio, and television. And if he happens to be on the northeast corner of Sunset Boulevard and Vine Street, he may notice a star with the name: KLAUS LANDSBERG.

He may pause there for a moment and wonder. “Who was THAT guy? Never heard of him.”

“I guess he must be somebody,” his companion might add. “They don’t just give these out to anybody. Do they?

-30-

SOURCE NOTES

Much of this book is based on my personal memories, and extensive files about Klaus Landsberg gathered over the years, as well as hours of personal interviews with members of Klaus's team at KTLA. Individual recollections were also recorded at a nostalgic Reunion of KTLA co-workers hosted in 1985 by my son Cleve and his wife, Catherine.

We have also relied on engineer John Silva's meticulous records of the station's early years, accessed at the website (emmysfoundation.org) along with a huge trove of photographs. Many images were also provided by producer Joel Tator, Eddie Resnick, family members, and Nora Bates of the Television Academy Foundation.

My co-author, George Lewis was helped in his research by the people at the Tehachapi Heritage League, the San Marino Historical Society, the Hagley Museum and the Los Angeles Public Library.

Following is a list by chapter of a few of the newspaper and magazine articles and other sources we consulted.

Some of the material for Chapter 13, "They Said it Couldn't be done," was drawn from the accounts of Charter Heslep, former chief of the Radio-Television branch of the U.S. Atomic Energy Commission -- "The Story of the First Live Televising of an Atomic

Detonation" -- an address delivered by Heslep at the University of Georgia on May 9, 1952. We also obtained access to letters from Heslep to his wife Margaret, archived at Oregon State University.

Also, notes provided by Dr. Jan-Christopher Horak, Director of the UCLA Film & Television Archive.

Listed below are a few of the newspaper and magazine articles we consulted:

1. A Mile High Proposal
   - "KTLA's Transmitter Set the Southland Pace," undated mid-1950's press release from station archives
   - "Wilson Peak," a National Geodetic Survey information sheet accessed online at www.ngs.noaa.gov/cgi-bin/ds_mark.prl?PidBox=EW1864
   - Speech by Klaus Landsberg at Writer's Congress, 1943.
2. Let the Games Begin
   - *Das Ferensehen in Deutschland* ("Television in Germany"), official pamphlet of the XI Olympic games, Berlin, Germany, 1936.
3. Passport to Freedom
   - New York World's Fair 1939 and 1940 Incorporated Records, New York Public library accessed online at: http://archives.nypl.org.
4. Go West Young Man

- Robert L. Pickering "Eight Years of Television in California" (June 1939)
- San Francisco Museum records www.sfmuseum.net/hist5/donlee.html
- Philo T. Farnsworth Archives – philofarnsworth.com
- "The Father of Electronic Television," (www.byhigh.org/History/ Farnsworth/PhiloT1924.)
- Harry Lubcke, "Birth of TV in Hollywood", *Variety* 75th Anniversary Edition

5. Performing Without a Net

- "Television—The New War Baby," *Popular Mechanics*, October 1943, 66-70.
- "Motion Pictures Classified by the National Legion of Decency," retrieved online at https://archive.org/details/motionpicturescl00nati

7. Opening Night

- "Commercial Tele's Debut Here Rates Low as Entertainment," *Daily Variety*, January 24, 1947.

8. A Deadly Brew

- Cecilia Rasmussen, "Deadly Blast a Proving Ground for Live TV," *Los Angeles Times,* August 17, 1987, B3.
- "Jury Lays Plant Blast to Dangerous Chemical Brew," *Los Angeles Times,* March 13, 1947, A1.

- Marvin Miles, "Plant Blast Kills 15, Injures 151-Mile in Downtown Area Wrenched," *Los Angeles Times*, February 21, 1947, 1.
- "Blast Held Worst in City's History: Huge Girders and Lengths of Pipe Hurled About Area Like Toothpicks," *Los Angeles Times*, February 21, 1947, 2.
- Scott Harrison, "Explosion at O'Connor Electro-Plating Corp." February 20, 2012, accessed at framework.latimes.com/2012/02/20/explosion-at-oconnor-electro-plating-corp/#/0

9. Who's on First?

- Owen Callin, "KTLA Wins 5 'Emmies' at TV Awards Banquet," *Los Angeles Herald-Express,* January 24, 1951.
- "Settle TV War Over MacArthur," Los Angeles Evening Herald-Express, April 13, 1951, A-1.
- Bob Thomas,"Special Emmy Bash Sunday will look Back,," September 13, 1998, retrieved online at http://community.seattletimes.nwsource.com/archive
- Evelyn De Wolfe, "Syd Cassyd Profile," *Emmy* magazine, April 1999.
- "1951: Microwave Radio-Relay Skyway," AT&T article retrieved online at http://www.corp.att.com/attlabs/reputation/timeline/51microwave.html

10. Everyone's Child

- "Girl Trapped Deep in Old Well," *Los Angeles Times*, April 9, 1949, 1.
- "Life Drama Unfolds as Crowds Gather, *Los Angeles Times,* April 9, 1949, 2.
- "Rescue's Chronicle of Heartbreak: Hour-by-Hour Account of Struggle to Open Deep Trap of 3 ½-Year-Old Fiscus Girl," *Los Angeles Times*, April 10, 1949, 1
- "Television Has 27-Hour Fire Trial," *Los Angeles Times,* April 11, 1949, 2.
- Evelyn De Wolfe "The Day Live TV News Coverage Was Born," *Los Angeles Times,* October 17, 1987, E-1

11. The Dream Team

- "KTLA...The Team," *Tele-Views*, January 20, 1950, 11.
- Frank Torrez, "Down Memory Lane With Dick Lane," *Los Angeles Herald-Examiner*, January 20, 1977, B-9.
- Myrna Oliver, "John Polich; Local TV Sports Pioneer," *Los Angeles Times*, June 1, 2001, B-15.

13. They Said it Couldn't be Done

- National Nuclear Security Administration, "News Nob," retrieved online at www.nv.energy.gov.
- Paul Henninger, "Landsberg: TV's Dynamic Pioneer," *Los Angeles Times,* September 16, 1966, 22

- Charter Heslep, "The Story of the First Live Televising of an Atomic Detonation, " an address delivered at the University of Georgia, May 9, 1952.

The following books and other publications also provided valuable insight:

- Stan Chambers, *News at Ten* (Santa Barbara, CA: Capra Press, 1994).
- Michan Andrew Connor, "Holding the Center: Images of Urbanity on Television in Los Angeles, 1950-1970," *Southern California Quarterly*, (Summer 2012).
- George Everson,*The Story of Television—The Life of Philo T Farnsworth*, (New York: Arno Press, 1974).
- Ed Harrison, "KTLA: Independent Station Supreme," *The Hollywood Reporter TV Preview 1984-1985,* 8-10
- "KTLA Anniversary Issue, *Tele-Views* (January 20, 1950).
- David Clay Large, *Nazi Games: The Olympics of 1936* (New York: W.W. Norton & Co., 2007)
- Museum of Broadcasting, *KTLA-West Coast Pioneer* (New York: Paley Center for Media, 1984).
- John Porterfield and Kay Reynolds, eds. *We Present Television* (New York: W.W. Norton & Co, 1940).

- "Program Poll Winners, *Tele-Views* (December 23, 1949).
- William L. Shirer, *The Rise and Fall of the Third Reich* (New York: Simon and Schuster,1959).
- Joel Tator, with the Museum of Broadcast Communications, *Los Angeles Television* (Charleston, SC: Arcadia Publishing, 2014).
- A Constantina Titus, *Bombs in the Backyard: Atomic Testing and American Politics,* (Reno: University of Nevada Press, 1986).
- Erico Verissimo, *A Volta do Gato Preto* [The Return of the Black Cat] (São Paulo, Companhia Das Letras, 1946).
- Susan K. Wilbur, "Television in Los Angeles, 1931-1952," *Southern California Quarterly,* (Spring, 1978), 255-270.
- Mark J. Williams, "*From 'Remote' possibilities to Entertaining 'Difference': a Regional Study of the Rise of the Television Industry in Los Angeles, 1930-1952,"* (Diss: USC 1992) dissertation, University of Southern California, 1992, accessed online at digitallibrary.usc.edu.

***

EVELYN DE WOLFE

Born and raised in Rio de Janeiro, Brazil, Evelyn De Wolfe first came to the United States on a student/ teacher fellowship to the University of Washington, Seattle.

Leading up to a life-long career in journalism, the University of Brazil graduate worked as a translator and interpreter for US government agencies in Rio, including the Coordinator of Inter-American Affairs and the Office of Strategic Services. In Hollywood, she was hired by Walt Disney as story researcher and later served as a Hollywood Foreign Press correspondent before starting her 40-year career as staff writer and columnist for the Los Angeles Times.

Evelyn traveled worldwide on numerous feature assignments with her husband, photo-journalist Leonard Nadel -- living with a Stone Age tribe in New Guinea; following medical missionaries in the Amazon, Africa, and Nepal; reporting on Bedouin tribes in the Negev Desert; hiking in the Himalayas; posting stories from Japan, Egypt, Australia, Greece, New Zealand, Ethiopia, Israel, and Lebanon. After retiring, she formed her consulting firm, Creative Backup. "Line of Sight" is her fifth book.

Evelyn was listed in Who's Who of American Women, picked up a few awards along the way but says her most gratifying achievement was performing as an honorary clown with Ringling Bros-Barnum&Bailey Circus and leading the Clown Band at its 100th-anniversary celebration.

She lives in Hollywood, has two children, two granddaughters, and three great-grandchildren.

***

GEORGE LEWIS

Looking back on his 42-year career with NBC News, George is reminded of the Johnny Cash song "I've been everywhere." His varied assignments as an on-air correspondent for the network took him to all 50 U.S. states and 30 plus foreign lands, including some very troubled areas.

He started his network career as a war correspondent in Vietnam, covered the fall of Saigon in 1975, the hostage crisis at the U.S. Embassy in Tehran in 1979 and the student revolt in Beijing in 1989. In Los Angeles, he covered the O.J. Simpson criminal and civil trials, the Northridge earthquake and 1992 riots that followed the Rodney King beating. His news reporting has won him three Emmys, the Peabody, and Edward R. Murrow awards.

A native Californian, George built crystal set radios as a Cub Scout and grew up watching many of the early KTLA shows. His fascination with television grew with time, and he wound up working
in local TV in San Diego while attending college in the early 1960's. His first job was as a page on a local show hosted by Regis Philbin at the NBC station there. George moved on to the newsroom at the CBS station, where he would stay until NBC hired him in Los Angeles.

During that time, George says he began hearing about Klaus Landsberg. "It has always fascinated me that no one had done a book about Klaus," he says. Now, years later, he welcomes the opportunity to be working on this personal memoir with someone who so closely witnessed the early development of West Coast television.

George lives in Santa Monica with his partner Cecilia Alvear. He has two daughters and three grandsons.

***

44910185R00116

Made in the USA
San Bernardino, CA
26 January 2017